THE CATHOLIC VIEWPOINT SERIES

Editor: John J. Delaney

John L. Thomas, S.J.

THE CATHOLIC VIEWPOINT
ON MARRIAGE
AND THE FAMILY

HANOVER HOUSE
Garden City, New York

Imprimi Potest: Leo J. Burns, S.J.
                   Provincial, Wisconsin Province

Nihil Obstat: John A. Goodwine, J.C.D.
                   Censor Librorum

Imprimatur: ✠   Francis Cardinal Spellman
                   Archbishop of New York
                   May 26, 1958

Preface

Family systems, like individuals, are all very much alike, yet all very different. This book aims to describe only the family system of the Catholic minority and to analyze some of the special problems Catholics are likely to meet in attempting to live up to their family ideals in American society. Catholic couples encounter many of the same family problems that others face under modern living conditions, but they must solve these within the framework of their own system of values. It follows that if we wish to understand their special difficulties we must know how they define the nature and purpose of marriage.

Hence, after stating the dimensions of the problem in Chapter I and its historical background in Chapter II, I proceed to describe the Catholic viewpoint on marriage and the family in the following three chapters. Next, because a family system depends not only on the inner logic of its doctrine but also on the cultural setting within which it evolves, Chapter VI offers a brief description of pertinent elements in contemporary American society. Finally, in the last two chapters I discuss the special family problems of the Catholic minority and the means required to meet them.

This small volume, like any book, reflects the contributions of many minds. I wish to make special acknowledgement to my former teachers, to fellow researchers in the field, to the publishers whose material I have cited, and to the Institute of Social Order, Saint Louis University, which financed my research and freed me for the writing of this book.

JOHN L. THOMAS, S.J.

Contents

Introduction

Of the various areas in which a difference between Catholic teaching and current American custom exists, none displays so marked a divergence as the field of marriage and family relations. In a society that numbered close to 400,000 divorces last year (almost a quarter of the number of marriages contracted in the United States) the Catholic Church teaches that marriage is indissoluble. In a society that tolerated an estimated 500,000–1,000,000 criminal abortions last year, the Church unqualifiedly asserts that abortion is murder. In a society in which the proponents of planned parenthood (that significant phrase for birth control, which Theodore Roosevelt called race suicide) are exercising greater influence by the dissemination of their propaganda, the Catholic Church proclaims that artificial birth control is an infringement of the natural law and a direct affront to Almighty God. In a society that considers marriage simply as a form of civil contract, the Church emphasizes its sacramental aspect and insists that the only valid marriage for her people is one performed before a priest. In a pluralistic society in which mixed marriages are not only tolerated but increasingly regarded as normal occurrences, the Church condemns mixed marriages and prohibits her children from entering into them without a special dispensation. In a society whose exploitation of sex and whose preoccupation with matters sexual has been the puzzle and wonder of the world, the Church emphasizes the dignity of sex while at the same time insisting upon its proper place in human affairs.

In short, in an activity that is fundamental to the race—the

9

propagation of the species—a minority, the Catholics, in American society holds fast to a set of standards that is opposed to, and in many cases diametrically opposed to, practices that are casually accepted as normal by that society. Since sex customs, marriage, and the family are so important in any community, it is obvious that the practices of any group that is at variance with the accepted customs of the society in which it lives might easily lead to dissension and controversy if those differing customs are not clearly presented and explained. At the very least, misunderstanding and consequent tension will develop unless the position of the minority group is made available.

In the case of marriage and the family it is a curious commentary on the American scene that, though the statistics I have quoted above would indicate that the general trend in this country is opposed to Church teachings in these matters, it is a fact that lip service is rendered by the vast majority of Americans to the ideals so vigorously maintained by the Church and her authorities. Even among people who firmly believe in divorce, the desirability of a firm family structure and the disastrous effect of split homes on children are widely recognized. The American society in general still has reservations about divorce though it indulges in it to the tune of nearly half a million a year. Marriage as a relationship between a man and a woman that will endure until death do them part is an ideal that the vast majority of Americans fervently desire. Basically, though the civil contract aspect of marriage is recognized, the great majority of Americans still believe that marriage involves far more than a mere legalism, even though they may not go so far as to consider it a sacrament.

In short, despite the fact that Church teaching on marriage and the family opposes the prevailing trend in American life, it is nevertheless a fact that, even among those people whose activities in this area directly contradict Church teaching, there is recognition that, if nothing better, the Church's teaching is a desirable ideal for many, however unattainable it may be in their eyes.

Since, then, there is this wide discrepancy between basic

Introduction

Catholic teaching in this field and general practice on the American scene, a book on this subject clearly stating the Catholic position has a definite place in the *Catholic Viewpoint Series*. The goal of this volume is to present in a logical and coherent manner Catholic teachings in the various areas affected by marriage and the family. It aims to present for Catholics and non-Catholics alike the basic teaching of the Church and the *reasons behind that teaching*.

This aspect of the book is of vital importance. Too many people regard Church teaching as merely the imposition of the will of a few cranky clerics on the Catholic populace, with a further attempt on their part to impose their arbitrary will on the whole American society. This book, I hope, will show that there is nothing arbitrary or illogical about the Church's stand on any of these positions. To the open-minded non-Catholic it will represent, I hope, a reasoned approach which will go far to explain that many of the Church's seemingly intransigent positions are based on firm grounds which are logical and rational. For the Catholic who has too often accepted the teaching of the Church in this field without bothering to know its source, it is our hope that this book will open up new vistas of knowledge and drive home to him the fact that in the final analysis all Church teaching may be traced back to our basic belief in the existence of a supernatural Being—God.

Catholics believe that we are made in the image and likeness of God, that we owe our existence to Him, and that all human actions must be related to Him. In the case of marriage and the family there is an even more direct relationship with the Almighty Being than with many other matters affecting man. If this book is able to present to non-Catholics an understandable exposition—whether or not they agree—of the Church's position in this field and if it is able to reinstate or reinstill in Catholics a basic understanding of their Church's teaching on marriage and the family, then it will, indeed, have served its purpose well.

JOHN J. DELANEY
Editor

THE CATHOLIC VIEWPOINT
ON MARRIAGE AND THE FAMILY

CHAPTER I

The Problem

One doesn't have to acquire in-laws to recognize that no two families are quite alike. Family attitudes, tastes, and ways of doing things differ on many subjects, from parenthood to parakeets, from paprika to plumbing. Some of these differences have regional origins. "Yankee City," "Deep South," "Middle West," and "Far West" still nurture distinguishing traits. Some derive from dissimilar national backgrounds. The American "melting pot" is gradually fusing differences, but cherished family patterns disappear slowly. Others stem from local situations. Farmers, urban cliff-dwellers, commuters from the suburbs, and modern nomads in trailer camps have each developed their own patterns of adjustment. Still others are related to social status. The "upper-uppers" differ from the "lower-lowers," and both of these in turn from those in the expanding "middle."

But all these differences may be relatively superficial, scarcely penetrating the complex set of essential values, standards, and conduct which constitute the elements of any operating family system. Most adult Americans are aware that more profound differences distinguish their marriage views and practices. These appear to stem primarily from diverse religious beliefs, though even among the unchurched there is little uniformity in this regard.

We have all been made highly conscious of special problems related to sex, marriage, and the family by recent increases in divorce, juvenile delinquency, and sexual freedom. Perhaps never before have these topics come in for such popular attention. We are daily deluged with talks, articles, and treatises on the so-called "crisis of the family" in the Western world. Yet a glance at the material reveals little agreement on the nature of this crisis.

At one extreme we find the rugged individualists who insist that our traditional form of monogamous marriage places excessive limitations on the development of personality. Although they are distressingly vague concerning the nature of this development they support what they call a "dynamic" view of the family, according to which the rights of the individual are supreme, while the use of sex, marriage, and the family is subordinated to wholly personal whims.

Others suggest that the present period of stress and instability is merely a passing stage during which the father-dominated family of our rural past is being transformed into the more desirable "democratic" or "companionate" type which will prevail in the future. They tell us we may well expect considerable disorganization while the shift is taking place, but the future is full of promise.

At the other extreme are those who judge all modern family changes only in terms of the past. They look with longing back to the good old days of our simple rural past and sincerely believe that most modern developments tend to disrupt healthy family life. In the same line are those who speak of a "sex revolution." They imply that traditional family values have been seriously undermined. What we are currently witnessing is not the formation of a new family system but the rapid disintegration of the old.

Such varied analyses clearly reflect the diversity of contemporary views on sex, marriage, and the family. As the experts tell us, our culture is pluralistic. Briefly, this means that American society includes a variety of groups embracing diverse religious beliefs, views of human nature, standards of conduct, and patterns of behavior. To be sure, American Catholics, Protestants, Jews, and the unchurched recognize a more or less common unity of outlook loosely called the "American Way."

Beyond this we are all free to develop our own systems of beliefs, norms, and practices.

But American society has always been pluralistic in this sense. Why are differences becoming so apparent today? Perhaps the chief reason is that during the past few generations we have been forced to adapt to the rapid changes introduced by extensive industrialization and consequent urban living. Basic differences in beliefs are brought so clearly to public attention when people must adapt to extensive changes in family life because, as we shall show, new patterns of conduct are necessarily devised in terms of underlying values and beliefs.

For example, if couples freely resort to the use of contraceptives whenever they desire to postpone, space, or limit pregnancies, their conduct logically implies certain beliefs concerning the meaning of sex and marriage. If marriage partners obtain a civil divorce and contract another marriage their action implies definite views regarding the nature and properties of the marital contract. Because the beliefs underlying our actions are seldom stated explicitly, we tend to forget that they exist, though they are necessarily implied in every intelligent program of action.

Even a relatively superficial analysis of the American scene reveals how widespread and profound current disagreements concerning the meaning of sex and marriage have become. To cite only a few examples, we do not agree on the meaning of marriage: Is it an institution based on the very natures of men and women and consequently expressing the Creator's plan, or is it a man-made affair to be tampered with, modified, and even eventually eliminated as society evolves? Many insist that marriage has no unchangeable purposes and functions, so that it can be manipulated at will.

We clearly do not agree on the nature of the marriage bond. Is it a sacred, sacramental partnership to be contracted permanently, or can it be dissolved by the state, mutual consent, or at the will of one of the parties? Church groups obviously differ in their views, while civil courts presume to dissolve the marriage bond as a contract scarcely worthy of serious investigation, provided the divorce action is uncontested.

We do not agree on the essential purposes of marriage. Is it a life partnership in which husband and wife seek mutual happiness and perfection by dedicating themselves to the procreation and education of new life, or is it merely legalized intimacy serving any additional purposes that the couple may choose? Many moderns place primary emphasis on companionship, professing to see no necessary relationship between marriage and children.

We do not agree on the moral laws regulating marital relations. Must the couple respect the normal physiological process of the marriage act, which they freely choose to perform, or may they interfere with this process in order to prevent possible conception of new life? Controversy over the public dissemination of birth-control literature, as well as the outspoken opposition to the use of contraceptives expressed by the Catholic Church and some of the smaller Protestant groups, indicates widespread disagreement in this area.

We do not agree on the use of sex outside of marriage. Must deliberate arousal and enjoyment of sex be confined to marriage partners, or may others, either alone or with another, make use of their sexual faculties as legitimate sources of pleasure? Opinions differ sharply here. Some speak of sex as play, while many regard it as a legitimate channel for expressing affection even outside of marriage. Indeed, with the exception of books written from a professedly religious viewpoint, there is no indication in most texts dealing with marriage preparation that the use of sex necessarily has moral implications.

What is the pertinence of these varied beliefs concerning sex and marriage? They serve to point out the special problems that members of a religious minority, striving to live according to their own specific moral code, will necessarily encounter in American society. As we shall point out in subsequent chapters, members of the Catholic religious minority embrace a distinctive, clearly defined set of ideals, standards, and patterns of conduct related to sex and marriage. The first step toward understanding their problems in this regard is to face the fact that great diversity of beliefs exists in our society.

Sooner or later most practicing Catholics are made aware that their beliefs related to sex and marriage differ in many important points from most prevailing views. However, many Catholics miss the profound implications of this diversity of beliefs. Because they tend to encounter these differences primarily at the level of conduct in the form of specific practices, they seldom reflect that differences in conduct logically imply differences in what people believe. Indeed, most Catholics tend to accept their own marriage views and practices without clearly recognizing that these stem from an underlying system of values comprising a distinct Christian philosophy of life.

This failure to grasp the necessary relationship between approved conduct and underlying values is bound to beget confusion and misunderstanding. Catholics tend to regard practices that they disapprove of as more or less willful deviations from proper moral conduct, forgetting that these practices may be based on different beliefs and consequently that what is really involved is a clash of two different philosophies of life. More important, Catholics who do not understand how their own family system is constituted, tend to regard approved Catholic beliefs and practices as little more than pious customs or outmoded solutions from the past. Under the pressure of modern living conditions and the example of others, they may simply "follow the crowd" and rationalize their action by maintaining that new situations call for new practices.

Because disagreement and confusion characterize contemporary American thinking on sex and marriage, perhaps we can best further define the dimensions of our problem by reviewing briefly what we know about family systems in general. This approach has the advantage of clarifying basic issues without getting lost in incidental, descriptive details. In the following chapters we want to discuss what is distinctive about the Catholic family and what problems Catholics will encounter in modern society. In order to do this, we ought to know what the family is, what it does, and how people derive the values they attribute to it.

What do we know about this human society called the family? In the first place, it is a universal human institution. As anthropologist Robert H. Lowie informs us, wherever we find men and women sharing community life, we find some type of marriage and the family. Everywhere it is a primary social group constituted by the community of parents and children. Although the family may vary considerably in form and activity among different peoples, several traits are universal. There is always some form of mating relationship through which men and women are brought together for purposes of procreation; there is some type of marriage ceremony or social rite by means of which this mating relationship becomes publicly recognized and is respected by the group; and there is always some arrangement providing for the economic needs related to childbearing and child rearing. Likewise, there uniformly exists a common residence or home, though this may not be reserved for the exclusive use of one couple; and there is some form of kinship system designating what blood or marriage relatives are significantly related to the spouses and how they are to be treated.

What does the family do? In every society it serves a dual purpose. On the one hand, it provides a socially approved means of regulating sexual behavior for purposes of reproduction. Because the sexual drive is so powerful every society has found it necessary to establish restraints and controls lest this impulse lead individuals to perform actions considered disruptive to the social order. The basic problem here consists in reconciling the need for control with the need for expression. Social order requires control; the survival of the group requires expression. Marriage has always been the key institution designed to achieve these goals.

On the other hand, the family provides for the development and education of children. Because human offspring are born helpless, requiring nurture, protection, training, and instruction during relatively long formative years, every society faces the task of providing for the care of children and the adequate transmission of its cultural heritage through them. Although in the past men have experimented with many types of social organization they have never found an effective substitute for parents. The loving attention and warm security required for satisfactory development of the child are offered only in the family. It is this complex of sexual, affectional, reproductive, educational, and economic functions that renders marriage and family life inevitable and universal.

History and the contemporary world reveal an amazing array of family systems. Though they all share the general traits and basic functions we have named, that may be about all they have in common. Among some simple agrarian societies of Africa and the Orient, for example, the family system may dominate political, economic, and social life while fulfilling a wide range of social purposes. In complex, highly industrialized societies like our own, it tends to assume much less social importance. Likewise, family systems may place major emphasis on the extended family circle composed of several generations of relatives or upon the immediate domestic unit comprising only husband, wife, and children. Furthermore, among various family systems the marriage bond may be regarded as absolutely stable, fairly stable, or conditional. It may also be exclusive between one man and one woman, or it may include various polygamous combinations. The position of family members may vary from relative equality to rather complete domination by the father or elders among the circle of relatives.

In other words, although the family must fulfill a set of necessary tasks in every society, men can devise various ways to achieve these purposes because they are not mere creatures of blind instinct. As the old Egyptian saying has it, "There's more than one way to skin a cat!" Different societies use different means to secure the fulfillment of essential family purposes and goals.

Unfortunately failure to distinguish these varied ways and means, which are changeable and relative, from essential family purposes and functions has led many moderns to conclude that there is nothing constant or permanent about the family. They describe the wide variety of family types existing throughout the world, list the many changes that have occurred in our own family system, and then jump to the conclusion that everything about the family is changeable and relative—the family has no essential purposes or functions; it can be anything we want it to be.

If our understanding of the family is to proceed beyond mere description and such superficial conclusions it will be helpful to recall an observation of William Graham Sumner, one of our first American sociologists. He pointed out that every social institution embodies both a structure and a value. Applied to the family, the term *structure* represents the means or ways devised to achieve family purposes and goals, that is, the pattern of relationships, the organized system of statuses and roles defining the expected modes of interaction among members of the family. The term *value* stands for meaning, that is, the basic definitions of family goals or ends, the way family members view the nature and purposes of marriage.

Thus, in describing a given family system we can talk either about its structure or about the values it stands for, but we should not confuse the two. Inasmuch as family structure represents the ways and means through which the family is organized and operates it will necessarily undergo constant modification in a rapidly changing society like our own. On the other hand, if family values are modified, this implies that people have revised their views concerning the very nature and purposes of the family. Indeed, in the final analysis it implies that consciously or otherwise people have revised their view of human nature.

This raises the important question of how we derive the values that we attribute to the family. What is the relationship between our definition of the nature and purposes of marriage and our view of human nature? We can see it clearly if we analyze any social institution. Such analysis reveals several elements of primary importance. At the very base we discover an underlying view of man, the human agent. This represents our answers to the following questions: Where does he come from? What is he? What is his purpose in life? Derived from the basic view of human nature are specific goals or objectives defining what essential human needs must be met if man is to survive and reach perfection. These goals represent the major values we think are worth striving for in the practical order. Finally, there are the social means or patterned procedures which we have devised to secure the effective fulfillment of these necessary goals. Custom, climate, resources, education, technological development, and so forth will affect the way we implement our goals in a given social situation.

Let us apply this analysis to the family. To start with, we can observe the pattern of relationships or interaction among family members at the level of daily conduct; for example, between husband and wife, parents and children, domestic unit and relatives, family and society. We can also note that these relationships embody and attempt to implement a definite set of marriage and family values. Family members feel that there is purpose in their activity and that they ought to act the way they do. Pushing our analysis a little farther, we discover that these purposes or values are derived from a distinct view of human nature and have been developed in the light of it.

Stated briefly, our analysis shows that if you want to know why people judge certain family practices to be right or wrong, you must find out how they define the nature and purpose of marriage. If you want to understand why they define marriage as they do, you must discover their view of human nature. In the final analysis, therefore, all definitions of human values are ultimately derived from some view of man, the human agent. If people hold different views concerning the origin, nature, and destiny of man they will logically define the nature and purposes of marriage differently and will develop different patterns of conduct in relation to marriage.

Because there is so much confusion concerning the proper use of sex, it will be pertinent to extend our analysis to consider how we arrive at standards or codes in this area. Obviously we will develop and regulate the use of our various faculties in accordance with the views we hold concerning the roles these should play in our lives. In regard to sex this means that we must decide what constitutes the right use of our reproductive faculty. What we decide will depend upon how we answer the following questions: What is the primary purpose or function of this faculty? What is its relationship to the total human organism of which it forms only a part? What is the nature of this total organism, that is, what is our view of the human agent, man?

Here again, as in our analysis of the family, we see that everything depends upon our view of the human person. All sane men can agree that the primary purpose of man's sexual faculty is the procreation of new life, for we can learn the purpose of a faculty by studying its normal and essential operations. But this knowledge in itself is not sufficient for establishing a moral code regulating the entire use of this faculty. In order to determine its right use we must also know the nature and purpose of the human agent of whom sex is merely a part or a property. For example, those who maintain that man is the end product of unknown evolutionary forces and wholly determined by biological or cultural factors will erect a quite different code from those who believe that man is created by God, a composite of body and soul, and endowed with faculties that enable him to distinguish right from wrong and to choose between them.

To complete our treatment of how family values are derived we must add a few words about religion. How does religion affect the formation of such values? Let us confine our observations to the major religious bodies of the Western world. Catholics, Protestants, and Jews base their religion on revelation. Although they may differ considerably in what they hold to be the content and interpretation of revealed doctrine, and even in their views on the nature of revelation itself, they all maintain the divine origin of their beliefs. If we analyze the content of their teaching we discover several elements related to marriage. All the major religions present a more or less clearly defined doctrine on the origin, nature, and destiny of man; some teaching on the nature and purposes of sex and marriage; and finally, fairly detailed and explicit codes related to sex, marriage, and family life.

Hence, throughout the history of the Western world religion has played a significant role in the formation of family values. Even though the sixteenth century marked an essential break with Christian family tradition by denying the sacramental nature of the marriage bond, the leaders of the Reformation continued to view marriage as a sacred institution offering the only legitimate channel for the expression of man's reproductive powers. Traditional American family values were likewise based on this premise. Some of the early colonists, to be sure, placed the marriage contract wholly under the jurisdiction of the civil authority, but they never doubted its serious, sacred character.

We can conclude that if confusion and conflict characterize American thinking on family values today, this must reflect either a reinterpretation of pertinent traditional religious doctrines or a gradual rejection of their influence on the formation of marriage and family values. Both forces appear to be operative. In regard to the first it is well to recall that the orthodox religious tradition of the past never doubted that the essential function of the churches was to serve as the means of reconciling dependent, sinful mankind to God. It conceived the essential human problem as man's need for salvation. In this context formal religion served not only as an instrument of salvation but as a strong disciplinary force unifying ethical theory and practice in men's lives.

There are indications that the American people have been so preoccupied with the conquest of nature and with efforts to adapt social institutions to ever-changing needs that they have come to regard the basic human problem as primarily one of adjusting to nature and to society. In this process organized religion serves a useful function by promoting the spirit of brotherhood and by interpreting man's constant efforts at the more efficient exploitation of nature as the fulfillment of the Christian ideal. As some religious leaders maintain, their theology has become "practical"; that is, it scoffs at "dogmatic subtleties and philosophical abstractions" and "gets things done." In this climate of opinion some religious leaders have not hesitated to reinterpret traditional religious doctrines to meet assumed contemporary family needs.

At the same time, some modern thinkers have denied that these doctrines have any pertinence to sex and marriage. A relatively powerful segment of the population regards religion as "unscientific" and non-rational. They conclude that religious beliefs should not influence the formation of family values and standards; rather, these should be based solely on the findings of modern empirical research. Unfortunately, since such modern social scientists tend to regard the human person as nothing more than a complex combination of basic urges, conditioned reflexes, and acquired habits, in whose behavior reason and choice play no decisive part, there is nothing in their highly selective findings that can logically furnish the foundation for a code of conduct or a consistent system of family standards. The best they can offer is a more or less objective description of what people are doing.

Throughout this discussion we have stressed the key importance of our view of the human person both in determining the nature and purposes of marriage and in formulating sexual codes, because contemporary confusion associated with sex and marriage stems primarily from lack of agreement in this area. The American people show by their actions that they no longer share the same views on the nature and purpose of man. As a result they do not agree in defining the nature and purposes of marriage or of sex. This lack of consensus concerning essential values and goals has facilitated the introduction of practices clearly destructive of our traditional family system. Although Americans still pay lip service to the Christian views of human nature and marriage they tolerate and promote practices based on quite different premises.

This paradoxical situation arises primarily because, as we have indicated, the views of human nature and of marriage upon which these practices are established are seldom made explicit. But what does our present divorce legislation imply other than a denial of the sacredness of the marriage contract? What does sexual freedom imply but the denial that this important area of human activity is subject to either right reason or the moral law? When modern popular reformers advocate so glibly such practices as contraception, sterilization, and therapeutic abortion, they never mention that these practices imply the belief that man is only a highly developed animal having no eternal destiny and no responsibility to God for his actions. In other words, they are advocating a set of practices that imply a view of the human person clearly opposed to the traditional Christian view.

Now that we have analyzed the manner in which values related to sex and marriage are developed we are in position to consider the special problems Catholic families will encounter in our pluralistic society. The coexistence of diverse views of human nature within a society assumes significance primarily to the extent that these views are relevant to the goals, norms, and conduct cherished by members of that society. As we have indicated, this relevance stems from the fact that views or images of man play a leading role in the genesis of marriage goals, the formulation of family norms, and the choice of conduct. At the base of every family system, at least in origin and early development, is found a distinctive view or image of man.

When discussing Catholic family problems we must keep constantly in mind that we are dealing with a religious minority attempting to live up to its distinctive family ideals in a society characterized by moral pluralism. Because the majority of Americans still tend to pay lip service to traditional Christian family standards, Catholics sometimes overlook the far-reaching implications of their religious minority position and the profound significance of the moral diversity that constitutes the climate of opinion to which they are daily exposed. American Catholics are living in a society that they have not made and over which they have only limited control. It follows that they have to operate within their own framework of values in terms of which they must develop their own "definitions of the situation" concerning appropriate conduct related to sex and marriage. Moreover, since they live in a rapidly changing society they will be faced with the constant task of interpreting new practices in terms of old principles.

In this connection it is worth observing that the Catholic family in American society assumes special importance as the primary transmission belt for the Church's distinctive values, norms, and patterns of conduct. In all societies the family serves as the normal social means through which religion makes its initial impact on the growing child. When a society is integrated—that is, when all members adhere to roughly the same system of values, norms, and patterns of conduct—this function of the family is enforced and supplemented by other social institutions when the growing child acquires new contacts outside the family.

However, in American society extra-familial influences may contradict, confuse, or fail to support what the Catholic child has been taught in the home. Under these circumstances the family becomes the primary transmission belt for the Church's distinctive system of values. If it fails in this, there is every likelihood that the coming generation will tend to "follow the crowd" in the society around them. This would tend to be true even if all children were trained in the Church's schools, for, as a general rule, Church and school can only assist the family in fulfilling this function; they cannot supplant it.

It follows that Catholics must rely primarily on their own initiative in securing the realization of their family ideals. Thus, considered as a religious minority, one of their chief problems is how to guarantee continued conformity to Catholic family standards by all members of the Church. Broadly speaking, the conditions necessary to secure conformity under such circumstances are adequate knowledge, sufficient motivation, and group support. Let us analyze these conditions briefly to see what problems they present.

In the first place, Catholics must possess adequate knowledge of the Church's family doctrine. Such knowledge implies both the clear formulation of family norms and their efficient dissemination among Catholics. The formulation of standards presents few difficulties because Catholics follow an organized, authoritative teaching Church. At times, of course, there may be some indecisiveness in the application of moral principles to new conditions, as we can see, for example, in the problems related to the use of rhythm or to the employment of women outside the home. Such instances are few and constitute no major source of difficulty.

The effective dissemination of knowledge, however, is not so easily handled. The chief social means available are the family circle, the Church, the private school, and the Catholic press. These institutions ordinarily complement each other in the teaching function. Ideally, what the child learns in the home is enforced by what he is taught in Church and school and by what he reads in the press. Unfortunately there is considerable evidence that Catholic parents are abdicating their roles as religious teachers in favor of the school. This has serious consequences even when children are able to attend religious schools, but since such schools are not available for an increasing number of children, their entire religious training will be confined to "released time" or the relatively brief instructions given before the reception of the major sacraments.

Church leaders also encounter their own teaching problems. In refuting the constant attacks against the Church's position on sex, divorce, and birth control they face the danger of emphasizing only the negative aspects of Catholic family doctrine, with the result that in practice many of the faithful lose sight of the positive. Further, there has been some failure to explain the necessary relationships between Catholic family values and norms of conduct, so that many Catholics retain a non-intellectual approach to religion and morality. They tend to be satisfied with practical conclusions and applications, showing little interest in the "reasons for the faith that is in them." For example, many can give no better explanation for "fish on Friday" than that "Catholics don't eat meat on Friday." The same non-intellectual approach is manifested toward chastity, marital morality, and so forth.

As we have indicated, in addition to adequate knowledge conformity requires satisfactory motivation. Catholic family standards impose difficult and exacting obligations upon the faithful. Of course one powerful factor motivating Catholics to follow their family standards is the fact that deviations are defined as serious sins. Further, these standards form a part of the total philosophy of life that has been developed in the normal Catholic from youth. Also, the Church imposes serious sanctions, such as the deprivation of the sacraments, in the case of some deviations. These sanctions serve as a constant reminder of the standards while they exert considerable pressure on the deviant to return to conformity.

On the other hand, several factors in American society tend to weaken motivation. As Catholics move away from their traditional centers of concentration and start mingling more extensively with others, many of their family standards are seriously challenged and may appear questionable to them for the first time. Moreover, the careless adoption of some current patterns of conduct in dating, living standards, and so on may increase to a burdensome degree the difficulties related to following Catholic family standards. At the same time, daily contact with individuals and groups who do not accept the Catholic viewpoint may easily lead to loss of religious convictions.

But even adequate knowledge and motivation are not sufficient to guarantee conformity. There must be support and reinforcement from others. On the positive side, in addition to support from members of their own faith Catholic couples experience solidarity with a considerable number of non-Catholics who conscientiously follow traditional Christian family standards. Furthermore, there is a growing awareness of the importance of family stability evidenced in public opinion and social legislation.

Nevertheless, lack of support appears in the failure of society to reward conformity and to withdraw esteem from deviants. Those who violate Christian family standards suffer no apparent loss of prestige and frequently gain considerable publicity.

Likewise, Catholics receive little support from others in working out suitable solutions to new situations which the family must encounter in a changing society. Because Catholics cherish distinctive family ideals they may not indiscriminately follow the family patterns developed by their non-Catholic contemporaries to meet change. This statement is obvious when applied to such practices as contraception, sterilization, abortion, divorce, pre- and extra-marital intercourse, and so on. It applies with equal force to some dating and courtship practices, fashions in feminine dress, forms of recreation involving the two sexes, conversation, reading, and entertainment. It is also pertinent to the hierarchy of social goals: physical comfort, avoidance of pain, "pursuit of happiness," accumulation of the material symbols of success, social prominence and acceptance are goals that hold subordinate positions in the Catholic system of life values.

The problems we have discussed up to this point stem primarily from within the Catholic group itself. However, there are other problems of an external character, that is, problems stemming from the minority status of Catholic families in a pluralistic society. Such problems are bound to arise from the very nature of marriage values themselves. The family does not operate in a social vacuum. It affects and is affected by other institutions to which it is related and upon which it depends for the fulfillment of its purposes. This means that a given family system, because of the values it seeks to realize, requires the existence of other related elements in the culture. These elements represent that complex of social conditions, attitudes, and patterns of conduct that are logically related to the effective implementation of distinctive family values in a given society.

For example, the adequate implementation of the Catholic view of chastity involves a specific set of social conditions: it implies a housing situation granting some degree of privacy, a community in which youth will not be perverted by evil contacts or bad example, reasonable freedom from public exploitation of the sexual drive, and so on. Further, it involves the development of pertinent attitudes, that is, adequate knowledge and appreciation of the personal and social significance of the sexual function in men and women. Finally, it involves the establishment of fitting patterns of conduct, that is, the prudent regulation and satisfactory channeling of the pertinent relationships between the sexes throughout life.

Why do Catholic families encounter special difficulties in implementing their ideals in American society? There are several reasons. As members of a minority Catholics are not in a good position to initiate, develop, or regulate the customs and practices adopted by society. This function is carried on chiefly by others, many of whom, as we have shown, hold views on sex and marriage that differ considerably from the Catholic system of values. We have only to consider prevailing social means associated with entrance into marriage (dating and courtship behavior), the control of reproduction (contraceptives), marital stability (divorce), the social regulation of the sexual drive (exploitation of sex through mass media), and so forth to recognize the problems Catholics face.

Further, family relationships affect each of us so intimately and have such far-reaching ramifications in the social order that they furnish a peculiarly fertile source of misunderstanding and conflict. Sharp differences may become apparent in interfaith marriages, social work, legislation, education, and community-service organizations. Unfortunately, when disagreements arise people seldom reflect that a clash of entire value systems is ultimately involved. Frequently such differences tend to be viewed as separate religious problems rather than as practical indications of diverse doctrinal systems. People say, "Catholics are opposed to divorce," or, "Catholics are against contraceptive birth control," as if these positions were based on mere disciplinary edicts associated with Church membership rather than specific applications of basic Catholic dogma.

Thus, when such differences arise both Catholics and non-Catholics tend to consider them apart from their context in an integrated system of religious beliefs. Misunderstandings are bound to arise when the premises upon which diverse practices are necessarily predicated remain obscure or unknown. Under these circumstances people tend to accuse those with whom they differ of irrationally refusing to adjust to changed social conditions, of stubbornly clinging to outmoded beliefs, or of undemocratically trying to force their acceptance upon others.

Finally, when Catholics attempt to secure the realization of those social conditions judged necessary for the effective implementation of their family system, their efforts are likely to be met with misunderstanding, misinterpretation, and even open opposition and conflict. People who do not share the same ideals will look with suspicion upon such efforts. For example, when Catholics vote against the public dissemination of contraceptive literature or when they support an organization like the Legion of Decency, other members of society are inclined to feel that such action results in an infringement of their liberty.

This remains a difficult problem in a democratic society. However, since the real source of disagreement derives from the conflict of opposing value systems, we will help clarify the human-relations problems involved if we state clearly the premises upon which such practical programs are based. Intelligent tolerance is not founded on hearsay or ignorance; rather, it seeks to know the truth and respects differences in the practical order because it sees them in relationship to a more comprehensive system of values.

CHAPTER II

Historical Background of the Problem

Family systems, like civilizations, have a history. They come into being, undergo modification, adjust to changes, prosper and endure, or disintegrate and cease to exist. Although the family as an institution is inevitable because of the necessary functions it fulfills there is nothing inevitable about a given family system. Since each is logically developed in terms of some view of man there can be as many different family systems as there are differing views of human nature. At the same time, even when people share the same concept of man and have similar views about the nature and purposes of marriage, their families may reveal many dissimilar characteristics. For example, the Catholic families of medieval France or England had many traits not found in contemporary French and English Catholic families, just as these families, in turn, differ from French-Canadian or American Catholic families.

This indicates that every family system embodies a central set of unchanging, absolute values distinguishing it from others, and a number of changing, relative traits resulting from the more or less adequate attempts to implement these values in a given society. For example, the set of unchanging, absolute elements in the Catholic family system is the permanent, indissoluble marital union of man and woman based on a sacramental contract and founded for the fitting procreation and education of children, mutual service, companionship, and so on. The changing elements are related to various views concerning the statuses and roles of husbands and wives, parents

35

and offspring, family units and extended kinship groups, family and society. These views are conditioned by the economic, political, and social institutions within which the family and its members operate.

It follows that in studying the history of a family system we must carefully distinguish its distinctive set of absolute values from its changing, culturally relative aspects. In the past two thousand years people from widely different social backgrounds have adopted the Catholic viewpoint of marriage. The families they formed may be dissimilar in many ways, but as long as they embody the basic values of the Catholic view they represent the same family system. On the other hand, when some or all of these values are rejected, as happened among the Protestant groups at the time of the Reformation, the result is a different family system, though it may take some time for this to become apparent. Likewise, the acceptance of family practices incompatible with essential traditional family values implies the development of a new family system, even while people may still pay lip service to the old.

Failure to distinguish between absolute elements in a family system and the varied implementations of these values in different societies has led many observers to classify family systems according to their external structure and traits rather than in terms of the meanings they represent to family members. This manner of classifying family systems deprives them of their intelligibility. It overlooks the values people aim to achieve when they enter marriage. It tells us little of how the marriage vocation is related to their total philosophy of life. For example, polygamy did not have the same meaning for the early American Mormons that it did for their Mohammedan contemporaries. Monogamy may mean many different things to various groups in the modern world. Consequently we must keep the distinction between absolute and relative elements in mind when studying the history of the Catholic family system.

As members of the broad cultural stream flowing from Western traditions, most Americans hold many marriage and family values in common. Ideally marriage is monogamous and for life. Marriage partners should love one another, be faithful, raise their children with care and affection, and thus contribute to the general welfare and the stability of society. Catholic couples share these ideals with their fellow citizens, but they differ from most in the conciseness and absoluteness with which they define their practical implications, while embracing additional values peculiar to Catholic belief. Because the Catholic position is so frequently misunderstood it will be well to explain its origin at once.

Like all Christians, Catholics derive their basic teaching on marriage primarily from three sources: reason, Scripture, and tradition. Through reason they arrive at the essential nature and purposes of marriage considered as a natural society. In Scripture they discover its divine origin and supernatural qualities. Tradition offers them the accumulated wisdom of centuries of Christian thought and experience expressed in more or less detailed moral codes and precepts covering the entire range of family relationships. However, Catholics differ from other Christians in the way they define and employ these sources in developing their views on marriage.

Undoubtedly the most distinctive doctrine that Catholics hold is their belief that Christ established a visible society or "church" whose function is to continue the work of teaching and sanctification which He began, and to whose consecrated rulers He gave the power to teach without error in matters dealing with faith and morals. Catholics believe that their Church embodies a living teaching authority which, under the divinely guaranteed guidance of the Holy Spirit, transmits the Saviour's redeeming message and rites down through all future generations. Hence, for Catholics the contributions of reason, revelation, and tradition are definitively interpreted and expressed by a visible teaching authority, who represents Christ in the hierarchy of the Church.

This belief in a Church with infallible teaching authority concerning matters of faith and morals significantly affects the

Catholic viewpoint on marriage. It assures uniform, universal, and changeless agreement concerning essential principles among the faithful throughout time and space. It offers Catholics absolute certainty in the defined elements of their marriage doctrine, since they believe the Church enjoys the constant assistance of the Holy Spirit. It guarantees the continuity and timeliness of Catholic doctrine. A living teaching authority serves not only to transmit the wisdom of the past, it continuously evaluates and interprets the present, applying old principles to new situations. As a result Catholics possess a concise, authoritatively defined set of principles and precepts covering all major aspects of family life.

Because some elements of Catholic marriage doctrine have been attacked as the fruit of mere theological speculation, it is pertinent to clarify matters at once by pointing out that the fundamental marriage doctrine of Catholics from the origins of Christianity to the present time has remained unchanged: marriage is a means of grace instituted by Christ to provide the family with the graces it needs. As we shall show, this was the belief of the first generations of Christians, and only a lack of historical knowledge could lead one to assert otherwise.

On the other hand, the explanation of Christian doctrine, preoccupation with heresies, and the attempt to state eternal truths in terms of specific philosophical or theological systems involved early Christian thinkers in a variety of disputes and controversies which must be evaluated in their historical context. In defending one point of doctrine they sometimes underemphasized others, so that by carefully gathering only selected texts from their writings one can prove almost any position. It will serve to keep the record straight if we outline briefly the stages of development through which the Catholic doctrine on marriage has passed.

When Christianity entered the Roman world it had no elaborate, clearly formulated family system to offer. Its first members were drawn from existing Jewish and Gentile family systems in which they had been reared and continued to live. However, the Church introduced a clear concept of the meaning of man and a definite moral code in regard to chastity, the equality of men and women before God, and the sanctity and indissolubility of marriage. The profound implications of this teaching were gradually reflected in a new family system representing a synthesis of existing practices with the new Christian principles.

We can study this early synthesis in the writings of St. Augustine (A.D. 354-430) and the Church Fathers. They taught the following points: First, Christian marriage was truly instituted by Jesus Christ. The primitive institution had become corrupted by pagan customs or by concessions to the Jews. Jesus restored it to its primitive purity. Second, in marriage husband and wife are assured the graces needed to fulfill their obligations. Third, Christ Himself gave marriage this sanctifying power. The Fathers saw in the Saviour's presence and first miracle at the marriage feast of Cana the first manifestation of this. Each marriage renews this sanctification, while the benediction and other ceremonies of the Church are its visible signs. Fourth, marriage among Christians is infinitely superior to pagan marriage. The Fathers found the source of this greatness in the statement of St. Paul that marriage is the image and symbol of Christ's union with His Church. As a symbol of this union marriage must be holy, one, and indissoluble. Fifth, the bond uniting Christian spouses was similar in holiness and permanency to the Christian's dedication to the service of God through baptism or the priest's consecration to the service of the altar through ordination. Baptism, marriage, and ordination are frequently compared in sermons and writing.

The essential continuity of Catholic marriage doctrine is clearly shown in Pius XI's classic encyclical *On Christian Marriage* (1931). In stating the primary benefits or goods of marriage the Pope goes back to the traditional formulation of St. Augustine: *fides, proles, sacramentum* (loyalty, children, indissoluble unity). *Loyalty* signifies that marriage is an exclusive union between husband and wife, rejecting as sinful any form of infidelity by either partner. The term *children* signifies that the primary purpose of marriage is the procreation and education of offspring, a privilege traditionally considered one of its greatest blessings. By *indissolubility* is meant the holiness and permanency of marriage stemming from the fact that it symbolizes the unity of Christ with His Bride, the Church.

The writings of St. Augustine, perhaps more than those of any other, influenced the Church's view of marriage down through the Middle Ages. The great theologian, St. Thomas Aquinas (1225?–74?), developed and clarified this traditional doctrine, while the Council of Trent (1545–63) reasserted it against the leaders of the Reformation. It is well to reflect that during much of this time the efforts of Christian thinkers were largely directed at Christianizing the pagan groups outside the Church, refuting heresies from within, clarifying official doctrines on original sin and the sacramental system, and formulating a body of positive law governing the marriage contract. It betrays a lack of historical perspective, therefore, to expect to find in much of the writing of that period the same conciseness and clarity of definition regarding marriage that exists today. The essential elements remain unchanged, but their integrated, definitive expression had to attend the development of doctrine in other areas.

Although toward the end of the Middle Ages court poets and popular writers made light of marriage and powerful heretical groups such as the Cathari and Albigenses in the south of France definitely rejected it, the Catholic viewpoint was widely accepted. Somewhat later, during the period of the Renaissance, the humanists began to discuss marriage apart from its theological context. While careful to avoid obvious heresy, in elegant and frequently satirical language they questioned the moral superiority of virginity over marriage, the status of women in society, the traditional roles of men and women in marriage, and so on. Much of this criticism perhaps merely reflected actual changes occurring in the social system, but the discussion of marriage outside its theological framework of values as expressed in the Christian philosophy of life indicated a naturalistic approach quite alien to the spirit of the Middle Ages.

The definitive break with traditional Catholic marriage doctrine took place during the Reformation. Both Luther and Calvin, the chief proponents of the movement, rejected Catholic marriage doctrine, and their teaching has dominated Protestant thinking in subsequent centuries. Luther not only denied that marriage was a sacrament but maintained that it was a civil affair and therefore its control and jurisdiction pertained to civil authority. He believed that marriage was a normal, physical necessity imposed by nature itself, so that vows of chastity were contrary to nature. Furthermore, since the conjugal act represents a physical necessity it would be against nature to bind spouses in a marriage that did not offer them mutual satisfaction. It follows that divorce should be allowed on a number of grounds such as adultery, impotency, refusal of conjugal duty, diversity of faith, bad character, and so on. Calvin also denied that marriage was a sacrament, though he regarded it as an honorable state of life and was severe in dealing with those who made light of it. Other Protestant leaders developed their marriage doctrine in the tradition of Luther and Calvin, contributing little that was original.

The Catholic reaction to this new teaching on marriage found expression at the Council of Trent, which solemnly reaffirmed the traditional teaching of the Church on marriage. At the same time the Council formulated legislation covering age at marriage, premarital investigation, publication of banns, mixed marriages, and various other conditions. With minor changes this legislation constitutes the juridical framework for Catholic marriage today.

Thus, the Reformation marks the introduction of a new family system in the Western world. On the one hand, we find the members of the Church who, in conformity with their traditional teaching, regard marriage as a sacrament and consequently as an institution under the control of the Church, which specifies the conditions for its validity and enforces its stability with supernatural sanctions. On the other hand, we find members of the Protestant groups rejecting the sacramental nature of marriage and consequently placing the contract under the jurisdiction of the civil authority, which claims the right to specify the conditions for its validity and dissolution. The far-reaching implications of this new marriage doctrine were not immediately perceived because the leaders of the reform made a great deal of the family as a natural institution. Nevertheless, once they denied the sacramental nature of marriage they opened the door to divorce, and in handing over the contract to the legislation of the state they placed the family at the mercy of changing philosophies of political power.

Inasmuch as the specific social implications of a religion depend not only on the inner logic of its moral doctrines but on the type of society in which they are applied, it will help us understand the problems of modern Catholic and other American families if we know something of the forces that have affected them in the past. Three main factors have helped to shape American families: the original domestic background of those who settled the country; the influence of the environment and the adjustments it required; and the rapid industrialization of the country, resulting in the family's transition from a rural to an industrialized urban setting. Let us consider briefly some of the pertinent aspects of these factors.

Perhaps the most important factor accounting for the diversity of American families in the past was immigration. The amazing growth of the United States has been the result not only of the high birth rate of the original settlers and their descendants but also of constant immigration. During the period from 1820 to 1930 this country received a gross immigration of approximately 38,500,000. Since not all of these immigrants became permanent residents of the nation the net immigration for the period can be set at about 30,000,000. The first influx of immigrants before the Civil War came largely from western and northern Europe. This has been called the "old" immigration as distinguished from the "new," which came largely from eastern and southern Europe and started arriving in large numbers about 1880. Although practically all the races and nationalities of the world were represented in our foreign-born population, Europe originally furnished the great majority.

The immigrants of course brought with them their own customs and traditions, and since they had a tendency to settle in separate groups their family folkways endured for some time. In general, immigrant families were patriarchal in structure. Their birth rate was relatively high, and their marriages showed marked stability even under trying circumstances. A degree of initial disorganization occurred among some of the national groups because of the disproportionate number of men in their ranks. During the period 1900–1909, for example, the ratio of immigrant men to each 100 women was 228. Given the immigrants' tendency to segregate in large numbers, this unbalanced sex ratio led to some increase in vice and demoralization for a brief period.

Closely interwoven in the immigrants' culture were their religious beliefs. Most of the original American colonists, with the exception of the settlers in Maryland, were products of the Reformation and accepted its marriage doctrine. Even at the time of the Revolutionary War there were only about 35,000 Catholics scattered throughout the colonies. As a result, later immigrants who arrived settled in a predominantly Protestant society. While the Protestant immigrants fitted into this cultural pattern rather easily, Catholics were placed on the defensive from the start. This led many of them to cluster around their national parishes—Irish, German, Polish, Italian, and so forth—as the nucleus of group activity and solidarity. These national parishes helped preserve the faith of the immigrant and still exert considerable influence on the religious life of many communities, although they are gradually losing their distinctively national characteristics.

The tendency of the Catholic immigrant to settle near those of his own faith and nationality has led to an uneven territorial distribution of Catholics throughout the country. Approximately 75 per cent of them are concentrated in 20 per cent of the territory. Roughly speaking, this is the area north of the Ohio River and east of the Mississippi region. The other 25 per cent are scattered throughout the remaining 80 per cent of the country. This means that the great majority of Catholic families are urban. Of the Catholic population as a whole, it is estimated that somewhat less than 20 per cent are classified as rural (farm and non-farm), while only about 8 per cent now live on the land as full-time farmers.

Although early settlers and later immigrants attempted to transplant their family patterns directly to the New World, they soon discovered that many adjustments were necessary if they were to survive or avoid complete disorganization. In the colonies and on the frontier the family was the basic economic unit of society; each household was forced to meet most of its own needs by itself. This required hard work, industry, inventiveness, and courage, particularly on the part of women, to whom fell the task of converting the raw produce of the land into usable products for the home. In reality there were many different frontiers as the settlers pushed westward across the country, but they were met with the same unbounded confidence in the future, the same eagerness to break away from the past, the same emphasis on independence and aggressive individualism, and the same disregard for social status based on hereditary rights. On the frontier every man had to prove his worth.

Under these conditions the traditional patriarchal family structure underwent considerable modification. The status of women tended toward greater equality with that of men because their work in the home was so essential and there were fewer of them. At the same time, young people learned to shoulder responsibilities early in life, and since the country offered them numerous opportunities, paternal control of their destinies was necessarily limited. These traits still characterize American families, though the conditions which produced them have long since disappeared.

One further historical change must be taken into consideration if we would understand the modern American family. This is the rapid industrialization of the American economic system. The result has been the movement of agricultural workers to non-agricultural pursuits and consequently from the farm to the city. In 1790 approximately 5 per cent of the population lived in cities of 2500 or over. In 1950 close to 60 per cent were city dwellers. The principal factors in this continued increase of urban population are the rapid growth of industry, which creates constant demand for industrial workers; a rising standard of living opening up new jobs in the service trades; better opportunities for advancement and for acquiring a higher standard of living in an urban environment; the low prestige value of rural occupations in an industrial society; and the advent of the industrial revolution on the farm, with the result that fewer workers are required to supply the agricultural needs of the population.

It is scarcely necessary to discuss all of the manifold effects of this rapid industrialization and urbanization on American families. Two points, however, merit attention. First, the structure of the modern urban family in an industrialized environment tends to change from the extended to the conjugal type. This is to say, less emphasis is placed on the extended circle of relatives and more on the small circle composed of husband, wife, and children. This change has important consequences for the family. In the traditional rural environment the immediate family of reproduction was part of an extended kinship system, with the result that members of the kinship group recognized a definite pattern of social rights and responsibilities among themselves. This strengthened the individual family unit and gave security to each member, for the extended family had resources not available to the isolated family unit. Today the conjugal family, composed of husband, wife, and immature children, stands alone and must face its problems with only its own scant resources to rely on. In case of marital troubles, sickness, accidents, and old age the state or some social organization must be called upon for aid. The individual domestic unit has no formal claim on the extended kinship group.

A second result of urbanization in an industrial environment is the increase of women in the work force. Since 1900 the number of women workers has increased from 5,000,000, or about 18 per cent of the total labor force, to around 19,000,000, or somewhat less than one third of the total labor force. The truly astonishing change, however, has been in the marital status of women in the labor force. During World War II married women workers outnumbered single women workers for the first time in the history of the country. This trend has persisted. Single women are now less than a third of the female labor force, whereas in 1940 they had been almost half. Married women, on the other hand, formed slightly more than a third in 1940, but constitute more than half at present. The percentage of widowed and divorced remained roughly the same in both cases.

Contemporary American families reflect all these aspects of their historical past. They are diversified, resourceful, and busily involved in adjusting to constant changes in their environment. The over-all picture is complex and shifting, but we can perhaps gain better perspective on our central problem if we single out a few pertinent characteristics for brief consideration. Granting that wide individual and regional differences exist, several traits appear more or less universal.

Families show a high rate of residential mobility. Americans have never been a people to stay put, and the disappearance of the frontier has not modified this trait. Each year a relatively high percentage of families change residence, move from city to city, from state to state. Recently, in all our major cities there has been a veritable exodus of long-time residents out to the suburbs. The vacuum thus created has been rapidly filled by migrants from other regions. The chief factors associated with this high rate of mobility are the desire for better living conditions, the search for jobs, and the increased use of the automobile as a means of communication. The result is a constant reshuffling of the population, the breaking up of old residential areas and the rapid formation of new ones, and the greatly increased interaction of members of different nationalities, beliefs, and family backgrounds.

Families also show a high rate of social mobility. Americans operate in a competitive, open class system which provides through its educational system the necessary ladder for advancement in an industrial society, and which hands out rewards on the basis of achievement rather than hereditary status. Young Americans are consequently motivated with the hope of raising their standard of living and advancing socially. Competition is admittedly keen, but there are always enough who make the grade to stimulate others to try. The one drawback is that even those who advance are never sure when they have arrived, for the "top" always remains one stage above them. Since there is no clearly defined standard of success the accumulation of material goods becomes the only accepted criterion, with the result that people tend to gauge their success in life by the number of material symbols they have acquired. In this atmosphere of upward mobility and competitive striving many traditional family values assume secondary importance.

Further, Americans are trained, enter marriage, and raise their families in a permissive, relatively tolerant, loosely integrated society. This means that our cultural "designs for living," as Linton would say, lack unity and consistency; our "blueprints for behavior" are confused and even contradictory. In matters of sex and marriage society offers no clearly defined rules as to what must be done, may be done, or must not be done but presents socially acceptable alternatives in each case, among which the individual is free to choose.

Although most people have been trained in terms of some definite system of values, the demands of education and employment, in addition to the results of residential and social mobility, force them to establish working relationships with such a vast variety of personalities, cultural differences, and value systems that they acquire a confused type of toleration for divergencies even in the field of morality. Living under similar conditions and facing similar family problems, they tend to regulate their sexual and marriage conduct according to group attitudes rather than inner, personal convictions. This tendency, together with the sameness in interests, styles, intellectual outlook, and standards of living promoted in advertising, education, the press, radio, television, and other means of communication, is producing a certain mediocre uniformity and "groupthink" mentality among all families sharing roughly the same socio-economic position.

What do we know about Catholic families in American society? As we have pointed out, because of their immigrant background and difference in religion they tended to remain segregated through clustering around their national parishes, highly urbanized, and regionally concentrated in the industrial areas of the East and Great Lakes region of the Middle West. Because a fair percentage of them arrived late, were relatively poor, and had to overcome the handicap of a different language, studies reveal that they rank somewhat lower as a group than Protestants and Jews in educational achievement, occupational rank, and socio-economic position.

More pertinent for our present study, there are clear indications that large numbers of Catholics are becoming highly mobile, are using education to mount the socio-economic ladder, and are moving to new residential areas to indicate their social success. They are anxious to better their own position and that of their children. As a result they are beginning to feel the full impact of middle-class pressures toward conformity, and because they are mobile they no longer enjoy the support and feeling of solidarity that their parents experienced in their more compact Catholic communities.

Closely related to the above in its effects is the mobility occasioned by the modern tendency to move out to the suburbs. Since Catholics are highly urbanized they participate in this movement perhaps more than others. Now as Catholic couples move out of their traditional communities and start mingling more extensively in American society, differences in family standards and practices are frequently experienced for the first time primarily as personal rather than as group problems. The individual rather than the group begins to feel the impact of secular ideals. Under these conditions, the problems of the Catholic minority are set in an entirely new context. Henceforth, individual Catholics must be prepared to face modern challenges to their value system on their own. This requires that they thoroughly understand the "reasons for the faith that is in them." Formerly, a feeling of group solidarity supported their loyalty to Catholic standards. As they move from relative segregation to fuller integration in an increasingly alien suburban culture, they are forced to make choices among competing family ideals and norms for which their previous training may have given them little preparation.

CHAPTER III

Marriage as a Way of Life

Before taking up the discussion of the formal definitions and juridical framework related to the Catholic view of marriage, it will be useful to consider briefly how Catholics look upon marriage as a going concern, a vocation, a way of life leading to happiness and perfection in the service of God. Of course for purposes of analysis we can and must discuss marriage under its sacramental, juridical, sexual, reproductive, economic, and educational aspects, but for the individual couple it appears primarily as a way of life. Husband and wife seek affection, companionship, security, mutual understanding, and support. They want to go through life together, sharing its joys and its hardships. They are not unmindful of the deeper implications of marriage, though they are confident that their love is strong enough to see them through whatever the future may have in store.

This manner of thinking is in line with the Catholic viewpoint. During the marriage service the couple listen to the following words: "May then this love with which you join your hands and hearts today, never fail, but grow deeper and stronger as the years go on. And if true love and the unselfish spirit of perfect sacrifice guide your every action, you can expect the greatest measure of earthly happiness that may be allotted to man in this vale of tears." Such solemn assurance of happiness implies a confidence in the vocation of marriage which can be warranted only if the Church considers marriage a divinely designed way of life leading to perfection. Her viewpoint can best be understood if we reflect how marriage is related to her total mission.

Catholics maintain that the mission of the Church is the same as that of her divine Head, Jesus Christ, Who stated, "I came that they may have life, and have it more abundantly" (John 10:10). With the coming of Christ a new power, capable of regenerating and re-creating humanity, was introduced into the world. In Christ man acquires a new nature and humanity is offered a new beginning; for by uniting the whole man—body and soul, sense and spirit—with a higher spiritual principle Christ makes of man a new creature. Hence the mission of the Church is essentially a restoration of humanity. Her work is creative and life-giving in the fullest meaning of these terms. Through Christ she offers to the world a new kind of life which alone is capable of transforming and absorbing into itself the merely human elements, that is, the physical and psychical forms of life that exist in man.

This restoring and re-creating mission of the Church implies a concept of human nature that steers a middle path between two profound misconceptions that have dogged the thinking of man down through the ages. Man is not a mere animal. He is not a pure spirit. As a unity or composite of body and soul he is a compound of both. His function in the hierarchy of creation is to stand as a bridge between the world of spirit and the world of sense. These worlds are both real. They are both created by God and consequently good.

As a composite of body and soul man is capable of receiving impressions from both worlds. He is in contact with the physical world about him through the sense organs of touch, sight, taste, smell, and hearing; while as a rational creature he is conscious of a twofold activity, knowing and willing. By means of his intellect he is capable of using the data supplied by the senses to arrive at knowledge of the nature of things. He is likewise capable of forming concepts, formulating judgments, and perceiving the relationships between means and ends. In his will he is conscious of his ability to choose between different means to achieve a purpose and of his ability to choose to act or not to act in a given situation.

Furthermore, since man functions as a bridge between two worlds, the lower universe of beings depends on him in a very real sense for its spiritualization. By observing right order in using creatures he integrates them in the universal order of being intended by the Creator. Hence the re-creating mission of the Church extends to all of creation. By organically reuniting the whole of man with a higher spiritual principle, it restores the broken link in the orderly chain of created beings. Not only are the world of sense and the world of spirit brought into proper co-ordination in man, but as a result of this restoration creatures are now used as the Creator designed them to be used. Before the restoration they were abused, so that in the graphic words of St. Paul, "every creature groaneth and travaileth in pain" (Rom. 8:22).

This re-creating of humanity, which is the essential mission of the Church, operates through grace. Man is "born again"; he becomes a "new creature" by sharing in the divine life of Christ. This higher form of life gives him an additional source of operation. He becomes capable of supernatural acts. But this new life, although it has been added as a gift and consequently can be separated from his natural life, does not exist as something "alongside of" or apart from his human nature. Rather, sanctifying grace elevates, permeates, and informs the whole man. In the "new creature" the supernatural order completely pervades the natural, although it may be separated from it by serious sin.

It follows that the life of the Christian acquires a new duality. Not only is he a composite of body and soul, but through sanctifying grace he now shares in the life of two worlds. The one, of which he is most conscious, he knows to be already dying. The other is the "world to come," being built up invisibly in the Mystical Body, in which he already shares through sanctifying grace. Because he has been reborn the Christian sees no necessary opposition between body and spirit, between Heaven and Earth. He is not tempted to embrace either the Manichaean opposition between the essential evil of matter and the absolute good of spirit, or the perennial secularist contention that the natural order is all that counts. Indeed, he sees that the most meaningful line of distinction must be drawn between unregenerated human nature—man left to himself—and human nature renewed by grace—man sharing in the Divine Nature.

Thus implicit in the Church's mission is the assumption that the basic issue facing man is his separation from God. At the very beginning of its history the human race was deprived of its participation in the Divine Life by a disorder of the will which sacrificed God to self. The effects of this original alienation from God have been perpetuated down through man's history. They have affected every facet of his nature. The human situation, as the Church conceives it, is man separated from God by sin. As a sinner man stands, as it were, in opposition to God. To solve this human dilemma the Church offers Christ, as victim for sin, as model, and as mediator between God and man.

Catholic teaching on marriage and the family must be viewed within this wider context, embodying a concept of the Church's mission, the nature of man, and the nature of grace. As a consequence it is based upon several fundamental postulates. First of all, everything created by God is good. Although the Fall deprived human nature of supernatural grace and participation in the Divine Life it did not destroy or intrinsically pervert this nature. Deprived of grace, man remains incapable of achieving his true purpose in life, but his human nature is not thereby vitiated or depraved. Rather, it stands in need of redemption, of supernatural completion through the restoration of union with God.

Further, grace builds upon nature. Although the supernatural extends immeasurably beyond the natural, it does not destroy it. However high above nature the Christian ideal may stand, its foundations remain rooted in the divinely established order of nature. The God Who is the model of all perfection is also the God Whose law is found in the created nature of things. The Word "by Whom all things were made" is also the Word Who came to save. Christ's mission was not to destroy but to redeem and complete—the Creator and the Redeemer are one God.

Finally, the divine plan for creation is revealed in the structure of the universe, composed of a hierarchy of beings that man can observe. By analyzing their operations he can discover their natures, and the study of these, in turn, reveals their purposes or ends. Hence human reason is capable of discovering the divine order in creation, and man must respect this order in making use of creatures if he is to achieve his perfection and purpose in life.

With these observations in mind let us turn to a consideration of marriage and the family. We want to know what God intended when He created man "male and female" and blessed marriage as the union of "two in one flesh" saying, "increase and multiply." Briefly, Catholics understand the divine plan as follows: All men are called to perfection in the knowledge, love, and service of God. Men and women who choose the vocation of marriage seek this perfection by mutually dedicating themselves to the service of new life. This dedication implies the exercise of their natural reproductive powers, the very use of which places them in special relationship to others as sexual partners and parents and to God as procreators. These relationships define the framework within which marriage partners must work out their perfection as persons.

In other words, when men and women enter marriage they form a mutually perfecting life partnership dedicated to the task of childbearing and child rearing. Hence marriage considered as a way of life involves the integration of the process of sex with the perfective processes of reason and grace. It will help us understand how these processes are unified to form an integrated whole in marriage if we analyze each one separately. Although they exist as parts or elements which acquire their full meaning only when seen in relation to the whole we can deal with them individually for purposes of study.

Sex stands for the sum total of organic and functional differences which distinguish men from women. Its specific characteristic consists in the possession of complementary generative systems, which gives the sexes a different relationship to the reproduction of the species. An analysis of the constitutions of men and women reveals that they are prepared to co-operate with the Creator in the production of new life. They possess internal organs for the preparation of the co-principles of life, external organs for the union of these co-principles, and in the woman's body is provided a protective environment in which new life can grow and develop until it is capable of surviving by itself. At the same time, experience indicates that men and women are normally endowed with a strong tendency to seek companionship in marriage.

It may be noted that the highly unique character of the sexual act itself derives primarily from the following sources: It is the act that profoundly and mysteriously unites husband and wife ("they shall be two in one flesh"). It is the act ordained by the Creator for the propagation of the species. The fruitful completion of this act requires the special co-operation of God, the Author of each new life. It follows that the reproductive organs and their use are clothed with a sacred character. The virtue of modesty prudently guards against their illicit excitation; the virtue of chastity regulates their use. Their misuse constitutes serious sin.

Thus, God Himself is the Creator of the specific differences between the sexes. He is the Author of the powerful inclination that leads them toward marital companionship. He has decreed the necessity of their sexual union for the propagation of the race. He has made them capable of enjoying the pleasures associated with their union. Nothing in the sexual life of man is evil in itself, for it represents a divine work. When evil occurs, it results from the use of sex contrary to the divine plan.

Furthermore, when the Creator specified the manner of human reproduction He *ipso facto* decreed the nature of marriage. Not only does reproduction require the union of husband and wife but the character of the newborn child is such that it requires the protection and guidance of both parents for many years. Hence, there must be some type of stable conjugal society, the establishment of a "home," and mutual support in supplying personal and family needs—affective, economic, social, educational, and so on. These needs, like the phenomenon of sex itself, are universal. They cannot be ignored or disregarded without serious consequences.

Neither the use of sex nor the development of the family results from mere "instinctive" drives within human nature. Man is a rational animal. As a unity of body and soul he acts through nature and reason. The profound attraction that develops between a man and a woman is not primarily the expression of a blind, inner urge. Rather, it is based on the knowledge and love of the other as a person—as another self.

To be sure, this attraction always includes the broad sexual element of manliness and womanliness, but in its initial stages at least, it does not focus directly on the generative aspect of sexual interdependence. This aspect appears as the completion or fulfillment of mutual attraction, so that among rational creatures the generative act is preceded and circumscribed by the knowledge and love of the partner as a person. Although reproduction gives marital companionship its distinctiveness and special quality it constitutes only one element of this companionship. Men and women form the marriage partnership as persons. This means they agree to work out their total life purpose together by dedicating themselves to the service of life. Childbearing and child rearing constitute the prime purpose of marriage, but marriage itself, like every moral association of men, is meant to serve the mutual perfection of its members.

Since this point is apparently misunderstood by some, it calls for further clarification. Although the primary goal that marriage partners must seek is their mutual perfection, to define marriage merely as a human companionship through which husband and wife seek personal perfection is quite deficient since it does not distinguish marital partnership from other partnerships between men and women. As a matter of fact, it is the procreative purpose of marriage that gives marital companionship its distinctiveness and specificity. The right to acts related to this purpose forms the substance of the marital contract. The psychophysical qualities that the capacity to perform these acts implies constitute masculine and feminine differences and are the source of their complementarism and mutual attractiveness. Furthermore, procreation is the basic reason for establishing cohabitation and the conjugal state. Hence even those acts of marital companionship which in themselves may not be directly related to childbearing and child rearing are implicitly connected with this purpose because they follow normally from the marital state.

To summarize our position then, men and women enter marriage in order to work out their perfection as persons, for this is the purpose of life. That which specifies or qualifies their companionship in marriage is its procreative nature. In other words, marriage integrates the process of sex with the perfective process of reason.

But marriage among Christians implies a further integration. As we have seen, the Christian is "born again," he becomes a "new creature" by sharing in the divine life of Christ. Through baptism Christians are united to Christ and privileged to share in His divine life as the branch shares in the life of the tree. In a very real sense Christians are wholly dedicated and consecrated to Christ. The intimate union with God which was lost through the Fall is restored through baptism. Christians are

Christ's, "purchased at a great price" by His Blood and bound by a total personal dedication of themselves to Him. This consecration to Christ in baptism is so complete that henceforth they live in, and for, and with Him. He is their first love, the source of their happiness, and the focus of their hope.

At first glance, marriage seems opposed to this complete dedication of self to Christ, for it necessarily involves a total personal gift of self to one's partner. How can these two complete gifts of self be reconciled in the Christian's life? Clearly, only if in reality they become one—only if, in loving and serving one another, each partner loves and serves Christ in the other. This calls for some explanation.

Although the total gift of self to Christ is clearly a spiritual act it must be tested and proved in the reality of human life. Love for Christ does not remove Christians from the circle of human obligations in which life places them. Rather, it increases the value of these obligations because in fulfilling them Christians show their love and service of Christ. Thus, married couples serve Christ through and together with each other. Their human love and fidelity toward each other do not conflict with their prior dedication to Christ but become the authentic sign of their love and fidelity toward Him.

Because they belong so completely to Christ through the redemptive sacrament of baptism it can be said that when Christians give themselves to each other in marriage they are, in fact, given by Christ. He stands behind their mutual gift, mingling His saving grace with their love and giving it the strength to endure "even unto death." In this sense the Christian who enters marriage receives a delegation from Christ—he becomes in his own person the minister of the Saviour's love toward his partner.

It follows that the process of grace in marriage may be considered under several different aspects. First, the perfection which men and women seek in marriage is Christian perfection. This is to say the primary purpose of marital love is that husband and wife "help each other day by day in forming and perfecting themselves in the interior life; so that through their partnership in life they may advance ever more and more in virtue, and above all, that they may grow in true love towards God and their neighbor" (Pope Pius XI, encyclical *On Christian Marriage*). The primacy of this purpose follows from the primacy of the human person in creation. In relation to it, all other finite purposes are secondary and instrumental.

Moreover, as we have indicated, marital companionship acquires its distinctiveness from its procreative quality. Through integration with the process of grace this noble privilege is marvelously elevated and "completed." Husbands and wives are now called not only to co-operate with God in the propagation and formation of the human race, but they become co-workers with Him in building up the Mystical Body of Christ. Through baptism their children become "sons of God" and "heirs of the kingdom."

Because their companionship is characteristically procreative, in terms of both the race and the Mystical Body, the framework of relationships which this function necessarily involves clearly defines the lines along which marriage partners must seek their perfection as persons. To repeat, there is no opposition between the vocation of marriage and the search for perfection. In Christian marriage the processes of sex and of reason are incorporated and integrated with the process of grace.

Finally, according to Catholic doctrine their marital companionship is founded on a sacramental base. Their calling to be co-authors and co-workers with God has been elevated by Christ to the status of a sacrament. The indissoluble bond that unites them becomes the source of the supernatural strength that they need to fulfill their calling. Nay more—through the sacrament the mutual love and service that characterize their partnership symbolize the union of Christ with His Bride, the Church. In this sense every Christian marriage becomes an exemplar and a symbol of that proto-Union through which all have received salvation.

This analysis of the three processes that must be integrated in marriage implies a view of conjugal love meriting further consideration. In reality men and women experience a double fulfillment in marriage. As human persons, representing two distinct images of God, they aid each other in working out their two irreducible vocations. As masculine and feminine persons, representing two incomplete but essentially complementary possibilities of human nature, they give themselves to each other in a mutually creative union. Thus, conjugal love, the mainspring of family relations, involves sexual, affective, and spiritual elements which must be properly ordered and appreciated if they are to be perfective of husband and wife.

There is a deep mystery in married love. According to the Scriptures, the union of two in one flesh creates a unique bond involving the entire person. In a sense the soul is given by means of the body. Husband and wife become two in one flesh so that each may regard the other as an extension of self, to be loved and cherished as oneself. This conjugal intimacy leads to mutual fulfillment, for it is a relationship in which the giving of self results in possession, and possession itself is a gift. By its very nature married love is directed both inward to the couple and, beyond them, to their extension in the child. This dual focus is so normal that it receives little attention, yet we here touch a profound truth of nature. As masculine and feminine persons husband and wife find essential fulfillment in the child. Conjugal love is doubly creative. It calls forth the full development of husband and wife, and it issues in a child, another human person.

Thus, the normal fruition of conjugal love involves parenthood. Through marriage husband and wife are caught up in the cosmic movement of the race toward continuity. But parenthood implies more than procreation. The human infant is born helpless, requiring nurture, protection, training, and instruction during long, formative years. Parents serve as the primary agents in caring for, loving, and "socializing" the coming generation. In particular, mankind has discovered no substitute for the family as the effective transmission belt for the accumulated values, norms, and understandings of the past which we call culture.

Further, in the supernatural order parents "build up the community of saints" by bringing forth children who will become members of the Mystical Body of Christ through baptism. By their example, guidance, and education parents become the primary agents through which these new members are effectively "Christianized" in the process of reaching maturity.

Finally, since man is a social being, seeking the satisfaction of his needs through co-operation with others in an established social system, parenthood necessarily binds marriage partners more intimately to their fellow men. In both the natural and supernatural orders it is children who effectively tie parents into the wider human community. The fulfilling process of parenthood is not confined to the family circle. Because they have children, parents are drawn to take an interest in the human community and in the Church, thus perfecting themselves as citizens of two worlds.

In this respect, marriage and the family perform an interesting function in the development of men and women. At marriage the intimacy of conjugal love breaks through the protective barriers of selfish individualism; then the narrow circle of "two in one flesh" is widened with the coming of children; and finally, the fulfillment of parenthood forces extension beyond the family group. When they have growing children, fathers and mothers soon discover that the local community, the neighborhood, the school, the church, the police force, public health, and other related matters take on new significance. The more perceptive are even drawn to take an active interest in the international community by the realization that their children may be called to serve their country in time of war.

CHAPTER IV

Marriage and the Church

Men and women fall in love, become engaged, enter marriage, and start building family life together so universally in our society that we tend to take the whole process pretty much for granted. This is perhaps as it should be. Marriage is a normal state of life, and boys and girls who have reached maturity in Christian homes should have acquired fairly adequate knowledge of what is expected of them as partners and parents in their own marriages. In this sense every family system tends to be self-perpetuating, for the family circle of the present molds and fashions the marriage ideals, attitudes, and aspirations of the future. Parents are models for their children in more ways than most of them suspect. By establishing a happy home and doing what comes naturally as Christians they transmit a living tradition.

We need not conclude that all formal definition and analysis of marriage is useless. Implicit in life in the Christian home is a set of ideals, principles, and precepts, which can be clearly formulated and defined. As we have indicated in the first chapter, what men judge to be proper conduct in marriage depends upon how they define the nature and purpose of marriage, and this definition, in turn, is related to their view of man. Moreover, both Church and state have vital interests in Christian marriage and have established legal codes governing the contract and its effects. The formulation of such codes implies a definite viewpoint concerning the nature and purposes of marriage, together with a definition of how marriage is related to Church and state.

A constant source of confusion in thinking about marriage

stems from the fact that it is regulated by two systems of law. Christians are members of two separate societies—the Church or ecclesiastical society, and the state or civil society. Through baptism Christians become members of the Church, the society established by Jesus Christ for the salvation of all men. By this membership they acquire new rights and obligations and become subject to the jurisdiction of the Church in matters pertaining to these rights and duties. The Church is interested in marriage primarily because it is one of the seven sacraments or channels of grace through which the merits of Christ's redemptive sacrifice are dispensed to the faithful. The Church's laws are stated in the Code of Canon Law.

Either through birth or naturalization Christians become citizens of the state. By their citizenship they acquire new rights and new obligations and become subject to the jurisdiction of the state in matters pertaining to these rights and duties. The state is interested in marriage as a contract having economic and social effects and as a reproductive unit rearing its future citizens.

This dual legal system gives rise to confusion and conflict if Church and state do not agree in defining the limits of their jurisdiction. Such a condition exists in the United States, where the various states assume complete jurisdiction over the marriages of their citizens. Contrary to the claims of the Church, the states maintain the right to define the conditions requisite for a valid marriage and the grounds for its dissolution. It follows that Catholic citizens must carefully distinguish between the requirements of canon law, which they are bound in conscience to follow, and those of civil law which may conflict with them. For example, civil law may accept as valid a union that canon law declares to be null and void. Catholics may obtain a civil divorce but remain validly married according to canon law.

It is of prime importance, therefore, to know how the Church defines her jurisdiction over marriage. Her position is clearly stated in Canon 1016 of the Code: "The marriage of baptized persons is governed not only by divine law but also by canon law, without prejudice to the competency of the civil power as regards the merely civil effects of such marriage." In practice this power of jurisdiction includes the imposition of conditions for the licitness and validity of the contract; establishing impedient and diriment impediments; judicial jurisdiction over matrimonial cases, even concerning the nullity of the bond; and enforcing observance of her laws by ecclesiastical penalties.

On the other hand, the Church maintains that the state has no direct or indirect power over the validity or licitness of the marriage of Christians. It is conceded the right to prescribe reasonable regulations for the protection of public order, health, and safety and also to pass laws governing the merely civil effects of the contract. Further, in regard to marriages between the unbaptized the state can lawfully establish impediments, even such as affect the validity of the contract; and prescribe other conditions, even affecting the validity, such as a requisite legal form for valid consent. It is generally held that the state has this power not as one of its proper functions but simply because there is no other competent authority to exercise it when the Church is not operative. Finally, when marriage has been or is to be contracted between a baptized and a non-baptized person, the Church claims the same jurisdiction as in marriages between Christians.

The Catholic position, both in defining marriage and in making laws related to it, is based on the firm belief that God is its founder. Pius XI stated this clearly in his encyclical *On Christian Marriage:* ". . . matrimony was not instituted or restored by man but by God; not by man were the laws made to strengthen and confirm and elevate it, but by God, the Author of nature, and by Christ Our Lord by Whom nature was restored, and hence these laws cannot be subject to any human decrees or to any contrary pact even of the spouses themselves."

The nature of marriage depends on the nature of man, and so long as this remains unchanged there can be no change in the nature and purposes of marriage.

It follows that we can learn the purposes of marriage and its essential traits by studying the nature of man. Reason shows that the primary purpose of marriage is the fitting procreation and education of children, and all its other ends are related to this purpose. We arrive at this conclusion by considering the existing order of created nature in which marriage appears as the only suitable means of providing for these ends in a manner befitting the dignity of men and women. Thus, we logically conclude that it has been designed by "God, the Author of nature," for this purpose.

We commonly use the term *marriage* to signify two different things. For example, we say, "Their marriage took place at St. Joseph's Church." Here the term stands for the act by which marriage is contracted. We also say, "Their marriage has been happy." In this case the term signifies the conjugal state or society resulting from the act. Canon lawyers recognize this double usage, speaking of marriage *in fieri* (the act) and *in facto esse* (the state). Their chief concern, however, is with marriage considered as an act because they are interested in determining the conditions for a valid contract. Marriage partners, on the other hand, are interested in marriage primarily as a state, since after the wedding they take the validity of the contract for granted.

How is the marriage contract defined? It is a legitimate agreement between a man and a woman conferring the mutual, exclusive, and perpetual right both to acts that are in their very nature proper for begetting offspring, and to the sharing of life together. Both canon and civil law recognize that marriage involves a special type of contract. The contracting parties are not free to specify its nature or contents; their freedom consists in choosing marriage as a way of life and in choice of partner. In most civil contracts the contracting parties can also specify the conditions and contents of the contract, that is, whether it is to be temporary or permanent and what rights it confers.

What are the effects of the marriage contract? It gives rise to a special bond between spouses which is by its very nature permanent and exclusive. In a Christian marriage, it bestows grace upon the partners provided they place no obstacles to it. It confers upon husband and wife equal rights and obligations in regard to those acts proper to married life. It binds them to live together, that is, to share "board and bed," unless some just, excusing cause intervenes. Finally, as parents they are placed under the strictest obligation to provide for the spiritual and material needs of their children. This includes their religious and moral education, together with adequate training for civil life.

Marriage considered as a state or society represents the actual living out of this contract. It may be defined as the legitimate union or society of a man and woman established for the purposes of generating and educating children, for mutual aid, and for sexual companionship. Hence the essence of the act of marriage is the mutual conjugal consent; the essence of the marriage state is the mutual sharing of conjugal life together.

The purposes of marriage appear clearly in these definitions. The primary end of marriage is the procreation and education of children; the secondary end is twofold: mutual help and the relief or remedying of concupiscence. Because these purposes are sometimes carelessly stated or simply misunderstood, they call for some explanation. To start with, it is incorrect and misleading to call procreation the primary end of marriage. It is procreation *and* education. The tendency to define it as procreation, even though education may be implied, stresses only one, and perhaps the less important, aspect of the primary end and leads to a misrepresentation of the Catholic position. As a result, non-Catholics sometimes conclude that the Church is interested primarily in numbers, while Catholics may take too lightly their serious obligation to establish the type of home in which their children can reach Christian maturity.

Further, the relationship between primary and secondary purposes is frequently misunderstood. Both primary and secondary ends constitute real ends of marriage, and the terminology signifies how they are related to each other. The term *primary* indicates that this is the purpose that specifies marriage and thus distinguishes it from all other societies. The term *secondary* signifies that "mutual help" and the "relief of concupiscence" exist so that "procreation and education" can be more easily and fully achieved and are consequently subordinate to this primary purpose. This relationship of order in no way lessens the personal importance of these secondary ends to marriage partners. It does emphasize what distinguishes marriage from other unions of men and women.

Misunderstanding has also arisen through failure to distinguish between the objective ends of marriage and the subjective purposes of those who enter marriage. The objective purpose of a thing is that toward which it is directed by its very nature. The primary and secondary ends of marriage which we have been discussing are objective purposes in this sense. Subjective purposes imply conscious motivation. In marriage they are the personal motives and intentions of the spouses operative in making and carrying out the contract. Although objective and subjective purposes may coincide in marriage, they need not do so. People marry for love, companionship, social status, economic security, to escape from home, avoid loneliness, and so forth.

The Catholic definition of marriage ends is sometimes ridiculed as unrealistic, because it is said that the majority of young people marry for other purposes. Such confusion of thought is possible only when people refuse to make or are incapable of making quite obvious distinctions. It is so widespread today because many deny we can know the nature of a thing from studying its normal operations. According to them we cannot conclude that the eye is made for seeing or a spade for digging.

Things have no objective purpose stemming from their nature —they are whatever we want them to be.

The marriage bond exists between one man and one woman and is indissoluble. These two qualities of unity and indissolubility are sometimes called the laws or essential properties of marriage. They are clearly implied in the definition of marriage we have just developed, so that their rejection signifies a rejection of this definition. Although some degree of marital infidelity has perhaps always existed even in the most Christian societies, the quality of unity has never been questioned among Christian nations with the exception of a few sects such as the Mormons. The quality of indissolubility, on the other hand, was rejected in the Eastern Orthodox Church starting around the ninth century, and by the Protestant groups at the Reformation. Hence these two qualities merit further consideration.

Unity signifies exclusiveness on both sides, that is, the bond unites one man and one woman. Monogamy alone places husband and wife on an equal footing in marriage; it alone offers the basis for moral union of intention and affection throughout life; it alone guarantees a type of family unity assuring a fitting environment for the training of children; it alone takes into account the profound meaning of the statement, "they shall be two in one flesh." This is so evident that polygamy has always appeared repugnant to those who think in terms of Christian values.

Some controversy has arisen among Christian philosophers and theologians concerning polygamy in the Old Testament. If polygamy is so contrary to the nature of marriage, why did God permit it among His chosen people? The answer is that we know very little about it. Scripture tells us that it existed but adds no comment. It praises the patriarchs primarily for their faith in the one, true God. In the creation narrative, monogamy appears as the primitive form of marriage. While the Mosaic code regulated rather than condemned polygamy, the practice disappeared under its regime. These are the facts in the case, and we are free to choose between the opinion that holds that God could dispense the patriarchs because polygamy is not opposed to the primary purpose of marriage, or that which maintains that God merely tolerated the practice, leading His chosen people by gradual stages from their corrupt practices to the perfect fulfillment of His law.

The quality of indissolubility signifies that the marriage bond cannot be dissolved by any merely human authority; that is, it cannot be dissolved by the will of the contracting parties or by the authority of the state. As we shall point out later, Catholics maintain that the Pope, as the Vicar of Christ, has the power to dissolve the bond under certain conditions. The Catholic doctrine of indissolubility is drawn from three sources: reason, Scripture, and the sacramental nature of Christian marriage.

The argument from reason is based on the nature and purposes of marriage. It is developed as follows: Since marriage is an institution that is indispensable to the development of the human race, it should be organized in a manner best calculated to secure both the continuity of the race and the happiness of husband and wife. From reason and experience it is clear that indissoluble marriage is best designed to achieve these ends, because the dissolution of marriage inflicts great harm upon children and because the mere possibility of obtaining a divorce places an obstacle in the way of perfect union and the desire to make the necessary inevitable adaptations required by normal family life.

Few people would deny that marital dissolution inflicts harm upon the offspring. However, some maintain that the mere possibility of getting a divorce has no effect on marital adjustment. They insist that a divorce is merely a legal declaration that a given marriage has already proved unworkable. This argument fails to distinguish between divorce considered as an individual act and divorce as an institutionalized social practice. As an individual act concerning one specific marriage, divorce may represent nothing more than a legal declaration of provious failure.

But when divorce is institutionalized, the implication is that the marriage bond is regarded as conditional. Under these circumstances people may enter marriage thoughtlessly, for the law offers them an easy out. They may refuse to make adjustments or assume responsibilities called for in the contract because divorce offers them an easy escape from facing the consequences of their acts. Finally, the presence of divorced persons in society poses a threat to stable family life. There are between 700,000 and 800,000 newly divorced persons in the United States each year. The majority eventually remarry, and since divorce is possible they do not hesitate to pick their future mates from an already existing marriage.

It is commonly objected that the doctrine of indissolubility places an excessive burden on unhappily married individuals. The sufferings of these "victim" cases are usually cited in defense of divorce. Such cases clearly deserve our sympathy, and we must do all that we can to lighten their burden, but we reject divorce as a solution precisely because it will increase rather than decrease the number of unhappy couples in society. Proponents of divorce cite these victim cases without paying attention to the unhappiness created by easy dissolution of the bond. In the final analysis we maintain that the family can best achieve its social purposes if it is based on an indissoluble bond. Since the social or common good takes precedence over the good of an individual, the marriage bond is indissoluble by its very nature.

Despite centuries of controversy over the meaning of certain phrases in St. Matthew, the argument for indissolubility in the Scriptures is beyond all reasonable question. This has been the constant teaching of the Church from the first century on, and it is difficult to escape the conclusion that only the desire to find some scriptural grounds for divorce has led Orthodox and

Protestant writers to question that Christ taught the absolute indissolubility of the marriage bond. At the same time, although scholars may well continue to concern themselves with textual difficulties, the major point of the original controversy, in which non-Catholics professed to find an opening wedge for divorce in Scripture, has lost its significance. At present the grounds for divorce have been so extended that references to Scripture scarcely appear pertinent.

The classic texts are as follows: We shall cite the Confraternity of Christian Doctrine's version in all cases. We read in St. Matthew:

"It was said, moreover, 'Whoever puts away his wife, let him give her a written notice of dismissal.' But I say to you that everyone who puts away his wife, save on account of immorality, causes her to commit adultery; and he who marries a woman who has been put away commits adultery." (Matt. 5:31–2.)

And later:

And there came to him some Pharisees, testing him, and saying, "Is it lawful for a man to put away his wife for any cause?" But he answered and said to them, "Have you not read that the Creator, from the beginning, made them male and female, and said, 'For this cause a man shall leave his father and mother, and cleave to his wife, and the two shall become one flesh'? Therefore now they are no longer two, but one flesh. What therefore God has joined together, let no man put asunder." They said to him, "Why then did Moses command to give a written notice of dismissal, and to put her away?" He said to them, "Because Moses, by reason of the hardness of your heart, permitted you to put away your wives; but it was not so from the beginning. And I say to you, that whoever puts away his wife, except for immorality, and marries another, commits adultery; and he who marries a woman who has been put away commits adultery." (Matt. 19:3–9.)

St. Mark's version of this incident is as follows:

And some Pharisees coming up asked him, testing him, "Is it lawful for a man to put away his wife?" But he answered and said to them, "What did Moses command you?" They said, "Moses permitted us to write a notice of dismissal, and to put her away." But Jesus said to them, "By reason of the hardness of your heart he wrote you that commandment. But from the beginning of creation God made them male and female. 'For this cause a man shall leave his father and mother, and cleave to his wife, and the two shall become one flesh.' Therefore now they are no longer two, but one flesh. What therefore God has joined together, let no man put asunder."

And in the house, his disciples again asked him concerning this. And he said to them, "Whoever puts away his wife and marries another, commits adultery against her; and if the wife puts away her husband, and marries another, she commits adultery." (Mark 10:2-12.)

St. Luke tells us that Christ told the Pharisees:

"Everyone who puts away his wife and marries another commits adultery; and he who marries a woman who has been put away from her husband commits adultery." (Luke 16:18.)

St. Paul is equally explicit; for example, writing to the Corinthians, he says:

But to those who are married, not I, but the Lord commands that a wife is not to depart from her husband, and if she departs, that she is to remain unmarried or be reconciled to her husband. And let not a husband put away his wife. (I Cor. 7:10-11.)

Any one who reads these texts with an open mind must conclude that Christ restored matrimony to its original indissolubility by abolishing divorce proper, that is, divorce with the right to remarry during the life of the spouse. This same prohibition concerning remarriage carried with it the rejection of polygamy, a practice allowed under the Old Law. In short, Christ restored the marriage bond to its original form of unity and indissolubility. His disciples clearly interpreted his teaching in this way and were not a little disturbed concerning its practical consequences: "If the case of a man with his wife is so, it is not expedient to marry" (Matt. 10:10–11). The early Christians never doubted that this was what He taught.

Controversy has centered primarily around the obscure phrase in St. Matthew, "except for immorality." Some translators use the term *fornication* here to translate the word *porneia* in the Greek text. Unfortunately we do not have the Aramaic original of the Gospel so that its exact meaning must remain obscure. At any rate it does not refer to a sin committed by one of the spouses with a third party, for then the Greek term for adultery, *moicheia,* would have been used. In the past Catholic Scripture scholars have maintained that the phrase applies to "putting away" or separation and does not limit the prohibition concerning remarriage. Since it does not constitute an exception to the universal rule it is not found in St. Mark, St. Luke, or St. Paul. Besides, if Christ had meant the phrase to signify permission for divorce on account of adultery, He would be contradicting Himself in this passage. Furthermore, He would have left His disciples in error when they questioned Him about it later.

Modern scholars suggest that the term *porneia* stands for concubinage or an invalid union. In this interpretation Christ's words would mean that a marriage may never be dissolved, unless it is not a real marriage; that is, unless it has only the appearance of one but is actually invalid. They point out that Greek, Aramaic, and Hebrew did not have a term distinguishing a married from an unmarried woman. Hence, Christ really said: "Everyone who puts away his *woman,* etc." Since this could be misunderstood, He added: "Except in case of *porneia* [that is, concubinage, an invalid union or no marriage at all]." Scholars add further that since Matthew was writing for the Jews, among whom concubinage existed, the phrase was necessary; Mark, Luke, and Paul were writing primarily for Gentiles, to whom the phrase would have been irrelevant; consequently they omitted it. Obviously this is a question to be settled by Scripture scholars. One point is clear: neither the Apostles nor the Christian faithful for centuries doubted that Christ taught the unity and indissolubility of marriage.

A third source of Catholic doctrine on this point is the belief in the sacramental nature of the bond when it is contracted between two baptized persons. Although it is held that unity and indissolubility are essential properties of all valid marriages, the sacramental character of the bond imbues these properties with a special firmness (Canon 1013). We shall see the reason for this doctrine when we consider marriage as a sacrament. It is sufficient for the present to indicate that it becomes pertinent in discussing the exercise of papal authority in dissolving the marriage bond.

We pointed out in Chapter II that one of the most distinctive and fundamental doctrines of Catholicism is that Christ established a visible organization or a Church to continue His redemptive work in space and time by teaching His message of salvation and dispensing the graces that He had merited. Furthermore, Catholics believe that Christ instituted a set of permanent rites, called the sacramental system, which constitutes the principal channels through which His grace is dispensed to men. In other words, there exist in the Church certain transactions of such a nature that they stand as visible signs of something spiritual and cause, confer, and contain what they signify. Hence, a sacrament may be defined as an outward, sensible sign instituted as a permanent rite by Jesus Christ to signify and effect by divine grace the sanctification of men. For example, in the sacrament or rite of baptism the pouring of water on the head of the recipient signifies the inner cleansing from sin and, in conjunction with the words of the rite, effects the bestowal of supernatural life.

Catholics believe that Christ raised marriage to the status of a sacrament. When marriage is contracted by baptized Christians capable of making the contract, this very exchange of consent through which the spouses pledge themselves to each other is a sign and source of special grace. In this case the contract is the sacrament, an outward sign of inward grace instituted by Christ. The ministers of the sacrament are the contracting parties, for they alone can supply the consent that makes the contract. The sacramental grace or supernatural aid made available to them is that which is required for a marriage worthy of Christians. Pius XI sums up Catholic doctrine on this point in his encyclical *On Christian Marriage.*

By the very fact, therefore, that the Faithful with sincere mind give such consent, they open up for themselves a treasure of sacramental grace from which they draw supernatural power for the fulfilling of their tasks and duties faithfully, holily, perseveringly even unto death. Hence this Sacrament not only increases sanctifying grace, the permanent principle of the supernatural life in those who, as the expression is, place no obstacle (*obex*) in its way; but it adds particular gifts, dispositions, seeds of grace, by elevating and perfecting the natural powers in such a way that the parties are assisted not only in understanding but in knowing intimately, in adhering to firmly, in willing effectively, and in successfully putting into practice those things which pertain to the marriage state, its aims and duties. It gives them, in fine, a right to the actual assistance of grace, whensoever they need it for fulfilling the duties of their state.

Among Christians the marriage bond remains a permanent source of grace, strengthening their unity, perfecting their natural love, and sanctifying them to the extent that they cooperate with it. Moreover, following St. Paul, Catholics see in the marriage bond a symbol of Christ's union with His Church, and consequently the sign of something eminently holy. A couple's love and affection for each other, expressed in the marriage bond, becomes a visible image of Christ's love for His Church, and just as the union of Christ and the Church is the efficacious cause of numerous graces, so Christian marriage, as a symbol and type of this mystical union, supplies the grace needed for Christian family life. Catholic couples are encouraged to keep this symbolism in mind, modeling their roles in marriage accordingly and recalling that through the sacramental bond they become the visible ministers of grace to each other.

Present Catholic doctrine on this point is clear enough, for the Council of Trent has officially defined matrimony as one of the seven sacraments instituted by Christ. However, since the development of the theology and formal definitions of the sacramental system was a gradual process, the accusation is sometimes made that the Church "invented" the sacrament of matrimony. The basis of this accusation is that Scripture does not speak of the institution of this sacrament and early Church writers did not use the term *sacrament*. This is quite correct. The present signification of *sacrament* is a relatively late development, since it implied advance and clarification in theological thinking. This does not mean, as we have shown from the writings of St. Augustine, that early Christians did not regard marriage as a means of grace.

In regard to Scripture, Catholics do not maintain that the institution of this sacrament is clearly mentioned there. They point out that St. Paul hinted at it in the Epistle to the Ephesians when he called marriage "a great mystery" (*musterion*), inasmuch as it symbolizes Christ's union with His Bride, the Church. It is to be remembered that the Catholic position is built on tradition, transmitted from the Apostles by a Church established by Christ with infallible teaching authority. As Pope Leo XIII insists in his encyclical *On Marriage, Arcanum Divinae:* "To the Apostles, as to our masters, are to be referred the doctrines which our holy Fathers, the Councils, and the Tradition of the Universal Church have always taught, namely, that Christ Our Lord raised marriage to the dignity of a sacrament . . ."

Finally, because there has been some misunderstanding of Catholic doctrine on this point, it should be noted that Catholics believe that all valid marriages between baptized persons, Catholic or non-Catholic, are sacraments. This conclusion follows from the fact that Christ raised Christian marriage to the status of a sacrament. On the other hand, marriage among non-baptized persons is not a sacrament though it is a sacred contract and has the same natural purposes and essential properties of unity and indissolubility as sacramental marriage. This conclusion follows from the fact that marriage is a natural society founded by the Creator for the fitting propagation of the race.

For purposes of comparison it will be helpful to give the view of marriage found in the civil law of the various states. The sacramental nature of marriage is not recognized in the civil law of the country. Civil law considers marriage in two ways, either as a contract or as a status in society. In the civil law of many states and in the judicial decisions of some courts it is stated that marriage is a civil contract and nothing else, but this seems to be taking the word in a very restricted sense. As many writers point out, matrimonial status or the conjugal state flows from the contract and is distinguished from it. Further, the matrimonial contract differs from ordinary civil contracts in the following ways: it cannot be rescinded by its very nature; the properties of the contract cannot be essentially modified by the mere agreement of the contracting parties; a juridical state arises from this contract; according to common law the two parties to the contract form one juridical whole; the requisites regarding the capacity of the parties to the contract differ from the requisites for making other contracts; and the marriage contract is not governed by that part of the Federal Constitution which treats of contracts in general.

Thus, it is clear that in civil law just as in canon law the distinction is made between marriage as an act and marriage as a society, or between the contract and the juridical state flowing from the contract. Although civil law does not consider the contract to be a sacrament, it does look upon it as a special kind of bond (*sui generis*). Further, there is a certain amount of agreement in regard to the properties of marriage. Civil law agrees with canon law in outlawing polygamy. However, it differs from canon law in regard to dissolubility. In civil law a marriage is indissoluble in itself but can be dissolved by a legitimate divorce granted by a civil court.

We have pointed out that because marriage is a sacrament the Church claims jurisdiction over the marriages of all baptized persons. Church laws regulating marriage are stated in the Code of Canon Law, the most recent codification of which went into force on May 19, 1918. The present Code represents the cumulative effort of nearly two thousand years of legislation. The Roman Rota, the Church's highest court of appeal, acts as its official interpreter through the decisions it issues on disputed points or doubtful cases. The Code is binding on the consciences of more than 400,000,000 faithful throughout the world.

Canon law covers three areas pertinent to the present discussion: it specifies the conditions requisite to the validity and lawfulness of marriage (the impediments), the nature of the consent in the contract, and the form of celebration of marriage.

Like all other contracts, the marriage contract consists of an agreement between two parties who are legally capable of contracting with reference to the object of the contract. If one or both parties are legally incapable of contracting, no real marriage results though they may go through the external forms. Such unions are called null, void, or invalid. In canon law the specific circumstances that render a marriage contract either illicit or invalid are called impediments. Hence, an impediment is a circumstance establishing a certain incapacity between two persons so as to affect the marriage contract itself.

The Code distinguishes two types of impediments: those that render the contract illicit or unlawful and those that make it impossible or invalid. It lists some fifteen impediments in all, but it is not necessary for our present purposes to discuss each of them in detail.[1] The Code admits the general principle that all persons can enter into a contract of marriage if not forbidden to do so by law. The right to marry is a natural right, not to be denied unless a valid prohibition of natural or ecclesiastical law can be proved. The natural law itself forbids marriage to persons who are incapable of the act which is the object of the contract or who lack the mental capacity to understand in a suitable manner the object of the contract. The pertinent impediments of the Code are as follows:

Age. According to the Code a man before completing his sixteenth year and a woman before completing her fourteenth cannot contract a valid marriage. These are the minimum ages required for validity and in no way represent an ideal. Rather, young people are encouraged to postpone marriage until they are fully prepared to assume its serious responsibilities. Of course societies throughout the world differ a great deal in regard to the age at which their members reach such maturity.

Impotence. In order to be capable of making a valid marriage contract, one must be capable of performing the marital act which is the object of the contract. One who is not capable of the marital act is termed impotent. The marital act, or conjugal copula as the term is used in this context, signifies the act by which semen from the husband is placed in the vagina of the wife by a natural act. Impotency must be distinguished from sterility, because sterility does not affect the contract.

Sterility is the incapacity for generation, that is, for procreating offspring. In practice one can make this broad distinction between impotency and sterility: whatever hinders the natural process of generation (capacity to have children) constitutes mere sterility; whatever hinders the human action of generation, that is, marital copula or intercourse, constitutes impotency. For example, if a woman has had her ovaries removed she is sterile but not impotent, because she is capable

---

[1] A relatively complete discussion of all the impediments can be found in *Marriage and the Family* by Clement S. Mihanovich, Gerald J. Schnepp, and John L. Thomas (The Bruce Publishing Company, Milwaukee, 1952), pp. 159–93.

of participating in the marital act and she is consequently capable of contracting marriage.

Existence of a previous marriage bond. If one or both of the parties seeking to contract marriage are bound by the bond of a prior valid marriage, they are incapable of contracting a valid marriage. Simply stated, until the previous bond is clearly dissolved, no new marriage bond is possible. Further, even though the previous marriage was invalid—that is, it was a marriage only in appearance—a clear proof of its invalidity must be offered before a new contract can be made. It follows that if either partner has been involved in any type of previous marital union they should inform their pastor of this fact when they consult him about their marriage services.

Mixed marriage. Catholics are forbidden to marry non-Catholics because such unions constitute a danger to the faith of both the Catholic partner and the children. The Code contains two impediments covering such marriages. One is termed "mixed religion" and renders *illicit* all marriages between Catholics and baptized non-Catholics. The other is termed "disparity of cult" and renders *invalid* all marriages between a Catholic and a non-Christian, that is, a person who is not baptized. If there are just and grave reasons for such a marriage, and if guarantees are offered that the faith of the Catholic party will be respected and that the children born to the union will be baptized and educated in the Catholic faith alone, a dispensation may be granted for a Catholic to enter such a marriage. We shall treat the whole problem of mixed marriage in a later chapter.

Marriage between relatives. Canon law regulates marriages between relatives. People may be related either by "blood" or by marriage. Blood relatives in the direct line—that is, when one descends from another—cannot marry. For example, marriages between fathers and daughters, grandfathers and granddaughters, and so on are prohibited. Blood relatives in the indirect line—that is, when neither person is descended from the other, but both are descended from a common ancestor, as are brother and sister—are forbidden to marry up to the third degree of descent inclusive, that is, up to and inclusive of second cousins.

Relatives by marriage cannot marry in the direct line of descent. For example, marriage between a man and his mother-in-law, daughter-in-law, and so on is prohibited. In the indirect line of relationship by marriage, marriage is prohibited up to the second degree inclusive, that is, between a man and his sister-in-law, his aunts or nieces by marriage, and so on. The appropriate authority may grant a dispensation from these prohibitions for certain degrees of relationship, provided just and grave reasons exist for the marriage. However, a dispensation is never granted for the direct line of blood relatives or in the first degree of the indirect line (brother and sister). They are seldom granted for relationship by marriage in the direct line.

These canonical impediments represent the principal factors that affect the capacity of individuals to make a marriage contract. They bind all who are under the jurisdiction of canon law. As we have indicated, a relaxation of the law in the form of a dispensation may be granted in particular cases provided due reason is demonstrated. Only the legislator or one who has received the power from him can grant such dispensations. Only the Pope has the right to establish ecclesiastical impediments, and he alone has the supreme and universal power to dispense from all of them. Power to dispense in some specified cases is granted to others either by common law or special papal indult. Conditions that are considered to arise from the absolute provisions of the divine law, for example, impotency, previous valid and consummated bond between baptized, and so on cannot be dispensed. Impediments of purely ecclesiastical origin may be dispensed although some of them never are, owing to their gravity.

The civil law of the various states also specifies impediments and conditions related to valid entrance into marriage. This legislation differs considerably from state to state, but it may be of some interest to take an over-all view of the principal laws that have been enacted in this area.

All states require that couples who wish to marry first obtain a marriage license. The license grants *legal* permission to marry. In most states it is issued by either the county recorder or a county officer. Most states require a waiting period between the time of the application for a license and the marriage. The average waiting period required is five days. Many states have a venereal disease law which serves the same purpose as a waiting period since results of the tests are not returned for several days. In many states the judge may waive the waiting period if the bride is pregnant or other circumstances appear to render the waiting period unnecessary.

A total of thirty-one states have venereal disease laws. These laws require a physical examination of both the man and the woman for venereal disease shortly before the marriage. This examination is good for a period of from ten to forty days depending on the various state laws. If marriage does not take place within that period, the examination must be repeated. In seven states the test is for all venereal diseases, in twenty-four states it is for syphilis only.

Interracial marriages are forbidden in about half the states, but the definition of what constitutes a "race" is very vague in most statutes. As a rule, intermarriage between Negroes and whites is prohibited in the southern states and between Orientals and whites in the western states. The constitutionality of these laws has been questioned and found lacking, but there seems little doubt that the pressure of unenlightened public opinion will keep them operative in many regions for some time to come.

All states have laws prohibiting the marriage of young people before certain ages. The states usually set two ages at which marriage may take place: one age that is legal if the parents give their consent, and one at which the young people may marry without parental consent. The most common ages for permitting marriage with parental consent is eighteen for boys and sixteen for girls. The most common minimum ages for marriage without parental consent are twenty-one for boys and eighteen for girls.

All states have some regulations concerning marriage between relatives. All states prohibit marriage between close blood relatives such as brothers and sisters, fathers and daughters, mothers and sons, and so forth. Twenty-nine states do not permit marriages between first cousins, or between half-brothers and sisters. About half the states have some regulations concerning marriages between various degrees of in-laws and step-relatives.

Finally, matrimony is declared voidable in many of the states if the presence of certain diseases such as epilepsy, venereal disease, or any seriously contagious disease is proved. A few states forbid the marriage of "paupers" who are living as charges of the public. A few states refuse to grant marriage licenses to "common" or "habitual" drunkards or to habitual users of "narcotic drugs." Several of the states have laws invalidating the marriage of perpetrators of major crimes, and in practically all of the states, condemnation of one of the parties for a serious crime is sufficient grounds for divorce.

Like all contracts, marriage can be effected only by the agreement or consent of the contracting parties. Valid consent, therefore, is required by the very nature of marriage. It follows that neither the state, nor the Church, nor any human power outside the contracting parties can supply the necessary consent for marriage. The reason for this becomes evident if we analyze the marriage contract. Every contract transfers some right, and the right it transfers is called the object of the contract. The Code defines matrimonial consent as an act of the will by which each party gives and accepts a perpetual and exclusive right over the body for acts which are of themselves suitable for the generation of children. Since it is an act of the will, only the contracting partners can give consent. Inasmuch as it involves the giving and acceptance of a right, some mutual expression of this consent is required by the very nature of the contract.

In order to enter any valid contract, the parties must be capable according to the law. The Code defines the factors that hinder true consent in the marriage contract as follows: want of the use of reason, defective knowledge of the object of the contract, mistaken identity, pretense or fictitious consent, duress and fear, and intention contrary to the essence of the marriage contract. When one or several of these factors as defined by the Code are present, there can be no true consent and consequently no valid contract. The general tenor of these obstacles to true consent is more or less self-evident. However, we should recognize that they are technically defined legal terms as used in the Code and must be applied accordingly in practice.

The civil law of the various states holds substantially the same view as canon law in regard to want of the use of reason, though in most of the states some sort of judicial procedure is required to declare the marriage null. In regard to mistaken identity civil law says very little, but the courts generally proceed in their decisions as if substantial error about the person invalidates the contract. Where the error was induced by fraud and is of such a nature that the deceived partner would not have entered the contract if the true state of affairs had been known, most of the states either by positive law or by judicial decisions of the courts maintain that the contract is voidable. Although many states have no specific laws dealing with duress and fear, the courts fall back on the common law, which holds such contracts null and void. In the states that possess positive laws on this matter the contract is considered either void or voidable. Finally, civil law makes no mention of conditional consent but assumes that the external expression of consent corresponds to the internal intention.

Certain conditions are required for the valid celebration of marriage. The Code defines the form of celebration as follows:

"Only those marriages are valid which are contracted before the pastor or the Ordinary of the place, or a priest delegated by either of these, and at least two witnesses" (Canon 1094). The aim of this legislation is to safeguard the liberty of the contracting parties and to have assurance that the marriage has taken place validly. It is to be noted that the officiating priest does not administer the sacrament; the two contracting parties administer it to each other when they make the contract. The presence of the priest is required as a witness representing the Church. Also, as a representative of Christ he blesses the marriage.

There was no universal legislation on the form of celebration affecting the validity of marriage until the Council of Trent in the sixteenth century. From the beginning Christian couples had been urged to secure the blessing of the Church on their conjugal unions, but marriages celebrated without the presence of a priest were recognized as valid sacraments, inasmuch as the contract itself was the sacramental sign. However, these unwitnessed or "clandestine" marriages were open to abuse. The contract could later be repudiated by one or both the parties, and it was difficult to establish with certainty the validity of the marriage when no competent person had been present to make inquiries concerning the freedom of the parties to marry and the existence of annulling impediments. In order to stop this possible abuse of a sacred contract the first invalidating law was passed by the Council of Trent in 1563 and after some modifications was adopted in the present Code. The law applies to all who are baptized in the Western Catholic Church. Catholics of the various Oriental rites and all non-Catholics, when contracting marriage among themselves, however, are exempt from its provisions.

The civil law of the various states requires that marriage be contracted in the presence either of a minister of religion or a duly designated public official. In regard to the necessity of witnesses, twenty states directly and expressly demand their presence for all marriages. The other states either require them for certain marriages or make no mention of them in their marriage laws.

The legislation of the Code covering capacity, consent, and form of celebration has been formulated to safeguard the sanctity and validity of the sacramental contract. With the same intent, specific practices dealing with marriage preparation have been promulgated. For example, the pastor must question each of the partners separately concerning the impediments, freedom of consent, and understanding of Christian doctrine to make certain that there are no obstacles to the contemplated marriage. Many dioceses of the United States require the couple to answer a set form or questionnaire covering the impediments and the usual obstacles to valid consent.

Further, the Code requires the publication of the banns. On three successive Sundays or feast days of obligation before a marriage is to be celebrated, the names of the contracting partners are to be announced at the principal mass, and the faithful are informed that they are gravely obliged to make known to the proper authorities any impediments or reasons why the marriage should not take place. The banns must be published in the parish church of each place in which the partners may live, and should they not be well known, in the parish church of each place in which they have dwelt for longer than six months after reaching the age of puberty. Only the bishop for just and grave reasons can dispense from the specified publication of the banns.

Finally, the Code requires the pastor to instruct the couple concerning the sanctity of marriage, the mutual obligations of husband and wife in Christian marriage, and the duties of parents toward their children. Since the law states that this instruction should be given "with due regard to the condition of the persons concerned," in those dioceses where pre-Cana or marriage preparation courses are commonly attended by engaged couples the pastor may have to do little more than personally assure himself that the couple have understood what they have been taught. In all cases it is customary for the couple to meet with the pastor for several instructions or discussion periods before the marriage is to take place. All of these requirements serve the further purpose of stressing the seriousness of the marriage vocation, and they obviously lessen the likelihood of those hasty, thoughtless marriages tolerated by civil law in some states.

Few points of ecclesiastical discipline have been more misunderstood and consequently criticized than those dealing with the administration of Church law concerning marriage. It should be obvious that it is impossible to understand the logic of the Church's stand on marriage if one does not grasp the concept of marriage that the Church teaches. It is rather unrealistic to suppose that the Church proposes one view of marriage in theory and another in practice. Those who have not taken the pains to understand the teaching of the Church on marriage run the risk of misunderstanding and misinterpreting her actions in dealing with actual marriage situations. The Church's administration of marriage laws is carried out in the context of specific definitions and rules carefully articulated in the Code, and it is clearly unscientific and unscholarly to attempt to evaluate it while ignoring this context.

A system of courts established by the Code for the universal Church administer ecclesiastical laws respecting marriage. The jurisdiction of these courts is limited to matters within the proper and spiritual sphere of the Church, and consequently the decisions of these courts have no civil effect but are binding on the faithful in the "forum of conscience." The Code provides for two types of court. The most important is called the annulment court, which through its various divisions deals with cases in which the validity of a marriage contract is in issue or a dissolution of the marriage bond is requested. A second court, called the separation court, may be established to deal with cases seeking permission to separate and live apart or to have recourse to the civil courts for a decree of separate maintenance or divorce. However, formal court procedure is not required in such cases, so that in most dioceses the bishop or one of his delegates handles them directly.

There are four divisions of the annulment court: the Roman court, the defect of form court, the documentary court, and the tribunal court. The marriage cases that they handle fall into two broad classes: cases petitioning for a dissolution of the marriage bond and cases in which the validity of the bond is in issue. Although an adequate treatment of how the annulment court functions is not pertinent here, misconceptions of what the court does are so prevalent among both Catholics and non-Catholics alike that a brief explanation appears in order.

Canon law uses the term *dissolution* rather than *divorce* in speaking of cases in which the bond of an existing valid marriage is set aside. Contrary to what is popularly held, the Church does dissolve a valid marriage bond in some cases. What about the Catholic doctrine of indissolubility? As we have shown, the Catholic doctrine maintains that marriage is by nature *inherently* indissoluble. This means that the marriage bond cannot be dissolved by any human authority such as the contracting parties or a judge in a court of civil law. Catholics also believe that a sacramental marriage bond (valid marriage between baptized persons) which has been consummated is absolutely indissoluble; that is, it is terminable only with the death of one of the partners. It follows that there is never any question of dissolving a valid *consummated sacramental* marriage.

On the other hand, Church legislation does provide for dissolution of marriage in the following four cases: unconsummated marriage, the privilege of the faith, unconsummated marriage in which one of the parties afterwards takes solemn vows in a religious order, and the Pauline privilege. Perhaps the best way to explain the Church's position here is to describe briefly what is involved in these cases and how the annulment court handles them.

In cases where a marriage has not been consummated and sufficient reason for seeking dissolution of the bond exists—for example, if it is impossible to reconcile the partners—one of the parties may petition for permission to start proceedings. If permission is granted, evidence in the case is taken locally and transmitted to Rome for consideration by a Committee of Cardinals acting as advisers to the Pope. Should this committee decide that the evidence in the case so warrants it the Pope may terminate the bond of the unconsummated marriage by a decree to that effect.

What are termed privilege of the faith cases also come directly under the jurisdiction of the Roman court. Cases falling in this classification arise when there has been a valid marriage between a baptized and a non-baptized person, and a subsequent breakdown of the marriage. If later one of the partners is converted to the Catholic faith a dissolution of the previous bond may be granted to allow the convert to marry in the Church. Two conditions are requisite: if it is morally impossible to reconcile the spouses, and if there is absence of scandal in granting the dissolution. Again, this privilege is granted only by the Pope, who acts on the evidence taken locally and transmitted to Rome.

There are the relatively rare cases in which the marriage is not consummated and one of the spouses wishes to take solemn vows in a religious order. The procedure is as follows: The religious order petitions the Holy See for permission to accept the individual as a novice. If permission is granted, dissolution of the unconsummated bond takes place when profession of solemn vows is made. It should be noted that according to canon law only certain religious groups are permitted to take vows technically defined as solemn. Such vows are usual among religious orders as distinguished from religious congregations.

Cases of the Pauline privilege occur when there has been a valid marriage between two unbaptized persons, the subsequent conversion of one of the partners to the Catholic faith, and the refusal of the non-convert to live in harmony with the converted spouse. Under these circumstances, dissolution is granted to allow the convert to remarry in the Church. The local chancery office handles the case and the procedure is as follows: In a letter stating the fact of his conversion, the convert asks the non-converted spouse two questions: whether he wishes to become a Catholic and, if not, whether he is willing to live peaceably in marriage without interfering with the religious duties of the convert. If no response is received within ten days, or if a negative answer is given to the second question, the convert may use the privilege. The bond of the former marriage is dissolved at the moment of entry into the new marriage. This form of dissolution is called the Pauline privilege because it dates back to St. Paul and his regulations for the early Christian converts at Corinth (I Cor. 7:2 seq.).

From this brief description of these four classes we see that they represent true cases of dissolution of the marriage bond. An existing bond is dissolved and the parties to the contract are granted the right to enter a new marriage. Valid marriages are involved, but it should be carefully noted that the marriage is either unconsummated or non-sacramental. Cases falling under the first three classes are not very numerous, but in missionary countries the Pauline privilege may be used frequently.

A second function of the annulment court is to deal with cases in which the validity of an existing marriage is in issue. In such cases the court is asked to investigate whether what purports to be a valid marriage ever existed. We have shown that according to canon law, marriage contracts may be null and void from the beginning because of some existing annulling impediment, or from lack of proper consent, or from a substantial defect in the prescribed form of celebration. A marriage is considered valid until proved otherwise. Should a supposed marriage later be found to be invalid every effort must be made to convalidate it by removing the invalidating causes. This obligation stems from two sources. First, since the marriage is simply null and void, the partners have no right to cohabit until the contract is validated. Second, although they are not validly married, they have acquired serious obligations toward each other and toward any children who may have resulted from the union, and such obligations can best be met by validating their union if this remains possible.

Unfortunately it is sometimes impossible to validate such unions. This may happen either because impediments exist which cannot be dispensed—for example, a previous valid bond —or because the parties refuse to live together. Under these circumstances the partner who has not been the cause of the impediment may seek a declaration of nullity. The Code has prescribed definite rules for dealing with all such cases, and three divisions of the annulment court, corresponding to three classes of possible cases, are delegated for the purpose.

Briefly, the *defect of form court* deals with cases that are null and void from lack of form. Such cases result, for example, when a Catholic attempts marriage before a civil official or a non-Catholic minister. The court judge, acting as the delegate of the bishop, receives the evidence; if it is conclusive he issues an official declaration that there has been no marriage because of defect of form. Doubtful cases must be remanded to the tribunal court for a formal hearing.

The *documentary court* handles cases depending on the mere presentation of documentary evidence relating to certain annulling impediments clearly stated in the Code. The judge of the court reviews the evidence and, after receiving the intervention of the "defender of the bond," an officer of the court with the duty of opposing the granting of a declaration of nullity in all such cases, disposes of the case in the light of the evidence. If the case remains doubtful, it must be handed over to the tribunal court.

The *tribunal court* deals with cases that, according to the regulations of the Code, require a formal trial for disposition. Once the court's jurisdiction is established the case is heard in the presence of from three to five judges and two special court officials, "the promoter of justice," charged with safeguarding the public interest and procedural law, and the "defender of the bond," who must oppose every application for a decree of nullity. If the court's decision is affirmative the case must be appealed to another diocesan court which has been selected as an appellate court. If this court gives an affirmative decision the declaration of nullity is granted. If the first court gives a negative decision the case may be appealed to the appellate court or to the Rota, the Church's highest court at Rome. Also, if the appellate court reverses the decision of the first court, the case must be appealed to the Rota. After the Rota studies the evidence, it hands down its decision and the case is closed except for the right to reopen it in the future if new evidence is offered.

This too brief treatment scarcely does justice to the complexity of the procedure involved. However, it is sufficient for present purposes to note that two affirmative decisions are required before a decree of nullity is granted. In this connection it is interesting to note the formula used in the decree. It does not state that the marriage under question was either valid or invalid; rather, it reads: the nullity of the marriage in this case is established, or, the nullity of the marriage in this case is not established. The decision is so stated because the judges must decide the case on the evidence presented, and they fully recognize how fallible they must be under such circumstances. It follows, therefore, that a decree of nullity does not dissolve a valid marriage. The decree merely represents a judicial decision on which the parties may act without sin. We conclude that it is morally wrong and spiritually futile for a Catholic deliberately to deceive or mislead the court, for a decree obtained in this manner would not justify remarriage.

Finally, because several declarations of nullity in the past have involved relatively wealthy parties some people appear to believe that "money talks" in annulment courts. Let us look at the facts in the case. Obviously court costs are involved, and the petitioners are expected to pay something if they can. However, the costs are ridiculously low when compared with legal fees involved in similar cases in civil courts. For example, annulment court costs in one of our large urban dioceses run as follows: If the case is heard before a one-judge court, costs are ten dollars; before the three-to-five-man tribunal court, the costs are twenty-five dollars, of which fifteen dollars are kept by the court of first instance and ten dollars are sent to the court of appeal. When cases must be appealed to the Rota in Rome, a charge covering advocate fees and printing costs is assessed.

If petitioners are poor they are granted the privilege of free hearing or a reduction of the ordinary fees. In no case is a petitioner ever refused a hearing because he cannot pay. For example, a study of the cases handled in a large American diocese shows that between one third and one half of all the plaintiffs were judged to be too poor to pay anything. Each year the Roman Rota publishes the number of cases handled, the nature of the decisions they received, and the number handled free of charge. Here again, over one third of the cases are annually judged too poor to pay court expenses.

We have seen that the marriage contract obliges spouses to cohabit. This normally implies the habitual sharing of bed, board, and home, together with the mutual companionship and assistance required for the adequate attainment of the purposes of marriage. Nevertheless, provision has been made for the cessation of this obligation to cohabit in those cases in which the good of one or both the spouses or of the children may require it. The right to cease cohabitation (separation from board and bed) must be clearly distinguished from the dissolution of marriage, or separation from the marriage bond. In early historical documents separation from board and bed was sometimes termed "divorce" (*divortium*), so that modern historians not acquainted with the strict terminology of canon law have sometimes drawn the erroneous conclusion that the early Church granted divorce in the modern sense of the term, that is, dissolution of the valid bond. Modern Church procedure may also cause confusion among the uninformed because Catholic spouses who are permitted to separate may be granted permission to obtain a civil divorce when the situation justifies it. From our previous treatment of the Church's position it should be clear that there is never any question in such cases of dissolution of the bond or permission to remarry.

Separation may be either temporary or permanent. The Code states that adultery on the part of one of the spouses, without breaking the bond, gives the offended partner cause for permanent separation unless the spouse consented to the crime, or had been responsible for it, or has condoned it expressly or tacitly, or has committed the same crime (Canon 1129). Tacit condonation is judged to exist when the innocent spouse, knowing of the adultery, has freely continued to treat the guilty partner with marital affection. Likewise, condonation is presumed if, within six months, the guilty partner has not been sent away, separated from, or duly denounced.

Even when adultery has not occurred, there may be good reasons why temporary separation should be permitted. The Code enumerates the principal conditions:

If one of the married parties becomes affiliated with a non-Catholic sect; if he gives the children an education which is not Catholic; if he leads a criminal and disgraceful life; if he is a grave danger to the other's soul and body; if his cruelty renders common life too hard; such and similar causes will give the spouse the right to withdraw by appealing to the ordinary (bishop) of the place; or even of his own authority if they are proved with certainty and there is danger in delay (Canon 1131).

These are grounds for temporary separation and should they cease to exist cohabitation must be resumed. Frequently they persist, however, so that what started as a temporary separation eventually becomes permanent.

According to the Code, petitions for separation may be handled in one of two ways. They may be heard directly by the bishop or his delegates, and the decision is then granted through an administrative decree; or they may be handled by a regular judicial procedure in which both parties are cited and their case is heard by one or several ecclesiastical judges, who then hand down the decision in the name of the bishop. Most dioceses follow the former method.

Whatever procedure is established, the general policy in dealing with petitions for separation is as follows: If there is any possibility of a reconciliation it must be encouraged, for the marriage contract obliges to cohabit. If reconciliation appears inadvisable at the time or if marriage counseling fails to effect it, permission for separation is granted. At the same time, the couple are reminded of their obligation to resume cohabitation when the grounds for separation cease to exist. This implies that they make a serious effort to remove existing obstacles so that they may eventually be reconciled. Finally, they are cautioned to avoid occasions, such as keeping company with others, that might lead to sin or become an obstacle to the resumption of married life together.

When may Catholic couples have recourse to civil divorce courts? Ecclesiastical legislation in force in the United States affirms that Catholic couples are forbidden to turn to civil divorce courts for permission to cease cohabitation unless they have previously consulted the proper Church authority. Also, they are directly and positively forbidden to seek the dissolution of their marriage bond in such cases. Furthermore, validly married Catholics attempting remarriage after securing a civil divorce automatically incur the censure of excommunication. Briefly, this means that until they have had the censure removed by proper ecclesiastical authority they are cut off from the life of the Church, may not receive the sacraments, and are refused Christian burial.

The Church grants couples permission to seek civil divorce in two types of cases. First, if the ecclesiastical annulment court decrees that a supposed marriage is in reality null and void, the parties involved may obtain a civil divorce in order to remove the civil consequences of the supposed marriage and to obtain *civil* freedom to remarry. Second, in cases of permitted separation when it can be shown that the innocent partner would suffer serious civil law disadvantages such as grave loss of substantial property rights, which only a civil court decree may remove, permission to seek a civil divorce may be granted. In some states a decree of separate maintenance may be obtained, and when this offers sufficient protection to the innocent partner ecclesiastical permission is restricted to it. The position of the Church on this point is consistent with her doctrine. Although they presume to do so, civil courts cannot directly or indirectly affect the marriage bond of the faithful. However, the state can legislate concerning the purely civil effects of the marital state, and consequently Catholics may have recourse to civil divorce courts when the situation justifies it.

Civil laws of the various states regarding annulment and separation differ considerably. In general the standard grounds for annulment are those concerned with the existence and manifestation of consent, and those concerned with the personal capability for marriage of the parties. The interpretation of these grounds in the civil courts are somewhat similar to those found in the Code, but civil law differs from canon law in regarding some conditions, such as impotence or marriage before the legal age, as constituting not void but voidable marriages; that is, the marriage is valid unless a decree is issued annulling it. Canon law regards such cases as simply null and void from the beginning.

Separation by mutual consent of the two parties is permitted in all the states, but this act has no judicial significance. Florida is the only state that forbids judicial separation; hence, every divorce granted there presumes to dissolve the marriage bond. About a dozen other states have no positive legislation regulating judicial separation, so that it cannot be obtained in these states. Seven states have laws regulating judicial separation in favor of the wife. All the others grant judicial separation for certain stated reasons. In all these states a decree of separate maintenance may be granted in favor of the wife.

CHAPTER V

Marriage and Morals

We are all conscious of the inconsistencies, contradictions, and irrationalities in our lives. We do not always do as we think. The humiliating gap between ideal and practice remains wide even in the best of us. The "ought" and the "is" do not always proceed hand in hand. With profound insight St. Paul graphically describes this tragic state of tension in the heart of man: "I see another law in my members, warring against the law of my mind and making me prisoner to the law of sin that is in my members" (Rom. 7:23).

Now the possibility of tragedy—and humor—in this human situation implies belief in an objective moral order which we can know and to which our actions should conform. Although history records the consistent gap between this more or less clearly perceived order and the deeds of men, it likewise testifies to the universal belief in its existence. But what happens when men reject or deny the reality of an objective moral order? When they regard all moral values as ephemeral and relative? When the frustrations and tensions they experience in trying to achieve their ideals are regarded as mere indications of failure to adjust and adapt their standards to an ever-changing situation? The result can be only confusion in society and personal negativism in the individual, compelled to follow without personal guiding principles of his own.

In our first chapter we indicated some of the differences that characterize current attitudes toward family morality. Indeed, we did not need two Kinsey reports to warn us that modern ideals and practices related to sex are confused and contradictory. Contemporary art, literature, and advertising reflect, even while they mold, a startling array of conflicting opinions and practices. Family theorists and marriage counselors appear to regard obvious disorganization as little more than regrettable "growing pains" in a period of rapid social change. Yet divorce rates and crime reports suggest that what was once considered socially pathological is gradually reaching the status of institutionalized normality.

This suggests that the *is* has been confused with the *ought*. What the majority of men do becomes the measure for judging what ought to be done. Moral standards are derived from majority practice; they are no longer based on absolute, unchanging principles which serve as the criteria for judging between right and wrong. This approach to morality is diametrically opposed to the Catholic viewpoint. Briefly, Catholics maintain that there is an objective moral order in the world based on the nature of things as God made them. We can discover the nature and purpose of things by studying their normal operations. Moral rectitude requires that things be used in accordance with the purpose expressed in their natures, for man, as a rational creature, must follow the order of right reason if he is to develop himself in conformity with his nature.

Hence, the moral law is that set of principles that specify and determine the conditions needed for the development of human nature, that is, the conditions under which man can achieve his end or purpose in life. We discover these by studying human nature, by analyzing the component elements of this nature and what they require for their development. It follows that, according to the Catholic approach to morality, the moral law is not an arbitrary set of rules and consequently subject to modification and change; rather, it is based on human nature and the conditions required to achieve its development and purpose. Because man is a rational creature his perfection is not achieved by the automatic working of instincts as among animals; he must control and direct his impulses and drives so that they serve his development and purpose in life. To the extent that he fails to do this he fails to develop and falls short of the perfection for which he was created. This explains St. Thomas Aquinas' saying: "We do not wrong God unless we wrong our own good" (*Summa contra Gentiles,* Book III, chap. 122).

In addition to this approach from reason, Catholic doctrine also specifies another source of moral instruction. Catholics believe that Christ established a visible Church endowed with authority to teach infallibly in matters of faith and morals. They have divine assurance, therefore, that the moral principles defined and taught by the Church represent God's law. Catholic philosophers and theologians may dispute about the application of these laws in specific circumstances—as knowledge of human nature and the conditions for its development increase, they may grasp more adequately their personal and social implications—but the principles themselves remain absolute and unchanging because they rest on the nature of things as God created it. In this sense there is room for development and growth in Catholic moral doctrine; there can be no possibility of change implying rejection or modification of essential moral principles.

With these observations in mind let us turn our attention to the Catholic viewpoint on marriage and morals. Because morality specifies proper conduct and because in our daily lives we are most conscious of differences existing at this practical level, the implications of the moral teaching we shall discuss in this chapter are more keenly experienced as sources of disagreement between Catholics and non-Catholics than the more speculative differences treated in the last chapter. Nevertheless, the former are clearly implied in the latter and stem from them logically.

Moreover, it should be noted that, though we must confine our treatment to moral problems related to sex and marriage, it would be erroneous to conclude that other areas of human conduct lack equal significance either for the development of the individual or the integrity of the Catholic moral system. Indeed, the basic moral principles applied here are relevant to all areas of human conduct, so that our treatment will furnish but one example of how Catholics develop their moral system.

When men and women enter marriage they seek happiness and fulfillment through the realization of their sexual complementarity. In the marriage contract they give to each other the mutual, exclusive, and perpetual right to acts that are proper for begetting children, while their resulting marital state represents their life companionship and partnership in the process of childbearing and child rearing. In other words, marriage places them in a reproductive state, and what specifies or distinguishes their marital union is its procreative nature.

This makes the concept of sex the starting point for any consideration of marriage morality. Marriage has meaning only in terms of sex, so that we must understand how people look upon this human quality and the conditions judged proper for its expression if we would evaluate their moral doctrines related to marriage and the family. The Catholic approach to sex starts from the knowledge of human nature gained by observation and experience.

Human nature, like most higher forms of life, is expressed disjunctively in men and women. While the physical and psychic traits of men and women are equally human they are not identical but mutually complementary. This quality of manliness and womanliness represents sex, taken in its most comprehensive meaning. Specifically sex denotes the possession of mutually complementary reproductive systems in men and women. Since man is a composite or unity of body and soul this property of sex affects all the elements of his psychophysical constitution. Because men and women are social beings and sex gives them a different though complementary function in reproduction, it necessarily affects their respective statuses and roles in the family and society.

All mature, normal men and women possess a complete though complementary generative system. In the life cycle these faculties normally develop and reach maturity with the development of the individual. Neither their possession nor development are matters for personal choice. They are sum and substance of each normal person, and through their physical, psychic, and social consequences they profoundly affect the development of personality.

Like all faculties those of sex possess what may be called a definite cycle of excitation. They are not always "in act"; that is, although they exert a constant influence on the human composite, in their use as specifically reproductive faculties they must be aroused by definite, appropriate stimuli. These stimuli vary widely, but the point to be noted is that they provide the basic means by which the use of these faculties is subject to human control. The individual does not have direct control over the development of his reproductive faculties; he has little over the cycle of excitation—that is, once the stimuli are present the reciprocal reaction of sexual arousal normally follows—but he can, at least to a considerable extent, select or regulate the stimuli to which he subjects himself.

What end or purpose do these generative faculties fulfill? We can discover this by studying their normal and essential operations. Such analysis reveals that their primary purpose is the procreation of new life, for in them men and women possess internal sexual organs which produce the co-principles of life (semen and ovum), external organs capable of effecting the union of these principles, and a sensitivity to various types of sexual stimuli designed to prepare them for the act of marital union. Furthermore, as mutually complementary expressions of human nature, men and women are normally attracted to each other, while through affection and love they are powerfully impelled to seek mutual fulfillment and the expression of their creative reproductive power by forming the life partnership called marriage.

From the Catholic viewpoint, therefore, the study of sex as it appears in human nature indicates that the Creator desires to associate men and women with His creative activity by making the propagation and education of the human race depend on their free co-operation. God appears as the Creator of the differences that characterize the sexes, of the tendency toward friendship and love which motivates them to unite, of the necessity of their sexual union for generation, and of the pleasures related to the fulfillment of this act. We conclude that nothing in the sexual life of man is evil in itself, for it manifests the Creator's plan.

Further, if evil exists it must result from the use of sex in a manner that hinders the development of human nature, that is, in a manner contrary to God's design. Moreover, since our study of sex reveals that its primary purpose is reproductive, it follows that all conscious or rational use of sex must be related to the fulfillment of this purpose. Man as a rational creature must realize the order of reason in the realm of sexuality as in all other areas of his conscious activity.

Hence, according to the Catholic point of view, when we state the conditions under which sex serves the development of human nature, or the conditions under which its use enables man to achieve his purpose in life, we uncover the moral laws that govern its use for men and women. The basic principle involved can be briefly stated: ". . . by the law of God and of nature, every use of the faculty given by God for the procreation of new life is the right and the privilege of the marriage state alone and must be confined absolutely within the sacred limits of that state" (Pius XI, encyclical *On Christian Marriage*). If by their very nature the purpose of the generative faculties is reproduction, with all this implies in terms of care and education of children, then there can be no doubt that the right and privilege of using these faculties must be confined to couples who by their mutual agreement have bound themselves to establish the kind of society in which children can be reared to maturity.

As a matter of simple fact no sane person either in the past or today has advocated reproduction outside the marital society. Everyone feels that children should be raised in a family, and modern research corroborates this belief with convincing arguments. Of course there probably always have been a few fringe individuals or groups who have advocated reproduction outside the family, but their experiments have ended disastrously and they have made little impression on the great majority of mankind. The real issues are whether all voluntary expression of the sexual faculties must be confined to the marriage state and whether in marriage the natural physiological process initiated by the sexual act must be respected, that is, whether it is permitted to perform the act while taking measures to prevent possible conception. Catholic doctrine on these two issues is clear and distinctive. Since it differs considerably from the views rather generally held in American society, it will merit more detailed treatment.

Moral principles drawn from reason and faith regulate the voluntary use of man's sexual faculties in the Catholic system. The sixth commandment, "You shall not commit adultery" (Exod. 20:14), and the ninth, "You shall not covet your neighbor's wife" (Exod. 20:17), furnish the scriptural foundations. Although the sixth commandment explicitly forbids only adultery it implicitly forbids all actions that either in intention or in fact normally lead to it or that are contrary to orderly procreation. All lustful thoughts and desires are forbidden by the ninth commandment. Thus, in these two commandments we find the basis for the Catholic position on chastity and modesty.

St. Paul, in his usual forthright manner, singles out some of the unchaste actions of his time for special condemnation:

Do not err; neither fornicators [unmarried persons who engage in sexual relations], nor idolaters, nor adulterers [those who engage in sexual relations between unmarried and married, or married persons other than the spouse], nor the effeminate [those who practice self-abuse], nor sodomites [those of the same sex who engage in unchaste actions together], . . . will possess the kingdom of God. (I Cor. 6:9–11.)

And a little farther in the same letter:

Now the body is not for immorality, but for the Lord, and the Lord for the body. Now God has raised up the Lord and will also raise us up by his power. Do you not know that your bodies are members of Christ? Shall I then take the members of Christ and make them members of a harlot? By no means! Or do you not know that he who cleaves to a harlot, becomes one body with her? "For the two," it says, "shall be one flesh." But he who cleaves to the Lord is one spirit with him. Flee immorality. Every [other] sin that a man commits is outside the body, but the immoral man sins against his own body. Or do you not know that your members are the temple of the Holy Spirit, who is in you, whom you have from God, and that you are not your own? For you have been bought at a great price. Glorify God and bear him in your body. (I Cor. 6:13–20.)

Catholic philosophers and theologians have developed a balanced, carefully defined set of principles related to sex. In their teaching, chastity is the virtue that moderates the use of the sexual functions in accordance with right reason, and as such it is a form of the cardinal virtue of temperance, which controls the human appetites having to do with the pleasures of eating, drinking, and sex. The chaste person is one who realizes the order of reason in the province of sexuality, while sins against chastity are transgressions and violations of the rational order in this area of human activity. As the term is used here, the "order of reason" is the order that corresponds to the reality made evident to man through faith and human knowledge. Now, considering the nature of man and his purpose in life, together with what we know about the generative faculties and their reproductive purpose, we must conclude that right reason requires that all voluntary expression of the sensitive appetite for venereal pleasure be excluded among the unmarried and be regulated in conformity with the purposes of marriage and the inherent purpose of the generative act in marriage. One who has acquired the habitual disposition to act in this manner possesses the virtue of chastity.

Furthermore, given the nature of man and the manner in which his generative faculties are stimulated to action, right reason requires that the various avenues that experience has taught may lead to transgressions against chastity must be protected and guarded. This is the function of modesty as it relates to the virtue of chastity. In this context modesty may be defined as that habitual disposition that impels one to avoid everything that is likely to excite venereal pleasure contrary to right reason either in oneself or in others. Inasmuch as the dangers that threaten chastity vary according to persons, times, and places, the specific requirements for the practice of modesty will vary accordingly. However, the essential purpose of modesty remains unchanged. It requires that we avoid those actions that common sense and experience show will either arouse or entail the danger of arousing venereal pleasure contrary to right reason.

Modesty implies a realistic, extremely practical approach to the realization of right order in sexuality. Taking people as they are, with all their variety of customs, dispositions, and aptitudes, modesty requires the avoidance of anything that arouses venereal pleasure contrary to right reason—not that venereal pleasure considered in itself is evil, but experience clearly shows that once this passion is activated it is likely to entice consent, thus leading to a violation of chastity. It should be obvious that the intelligent practice of modesty requires some knowledge of how venereal pleasure is aroused. Since men and women differ considerably in this regard, each sex should have some practical understanding of their own normal "cycle of excitation," as well as that of the opposite sex.

Finally, because the consequences of misunderstanding Catholic doctrine on this point are so serious, it should be emphasized that it is the conscious, deliberate choice to use one's sexual faculties contrary to the moral law which constitutes the sin of unchastity. The moral evil of the act is in the will by which man chooses to use his sexual powers contrary to right reason. Neither the sexual organs nor the human body with its natural tendencies, reactions, phantasms, thoughts, looks, touches, and so on, are evil in themselves. The resulting actions and desires become blameworthy only when they become the manifestations of a morally culpable act of the will. Failure to understand this point has led to a false interpretation of the Catholic concept of sin, together with the perverted attitude that everything related to sex is somehow impure, defiling, and beneath the true dignity of men.

We have seen that chastity excludes all voluntary expression of the sensitive appetite for venereal pleasure in the unmarried. This specific form of pleasure is normally associated with the excitation of the generative organs and the performance of the sexual act. It is an accompanying effect, rather than the objective, inherent purpose of the sexual faculties. As reproductive faculties by their very nature, their use is subordinate to the purposes of marriage, and any attempt to use them as sources of pleasure outside the marriage state is consequently contrary to the order of right reason. It follows that actions that seek venereal pleasure through voluntary self-stimulation or through stimulation with one of the same sex or between an unmarried couple are contrary to right reason and morally wrong. Intercourse outside of marriage also constitutes a violation of justice, for if one or both parties are married it is an injustice to the partner, and if they are both unmarried it is an injustice to the child who may result from the act.

The observance of chastity may give rise to special problems in our society for a number of reasons: the sexual drive is openly exploited through every avenue of communication; young people reach biological maturity several years before they are old enough to marry; prolonged and relatively intimate association between boys and girls is tolerated and frequently promoted; and young people receive little guidance and instruction showing them how to integrate their newly experienced sexual impulses and drives with the total development of their personality. Such conditions are scarcely conducive to the realization of the order of reason in sexuality among adolescents. As we indicated earlier, values have social implications. Chastity will be observed by the average adolescent only if the conditions normally required for its preservation exist in society; if these conditions are ignored the stimulus-reaction process in the normal adolescent sexual system creates demands that are not likely to be left long unsatisfied.

The final stages of courtship and the engagement period frequently lead to special difficulties related to chastity. Although the sexual reactions of individuals differ greatly some people encounter serious problems in control under the stimulation of mutual love and additional intimacy. The order of right reason indicates the following general principles are applicable under these circumstances. Engaged couples are permitted the manifestations of mutual affection generally considered normal in their situation. However, they are not permitted to seek sexual gratification before marriage and must refuse consent to any sexual impulses that may incidentally arise as the result of permissible demonstrations of affection. In practice, couples must learn to avoid any situation that threatens their moral integrity, keeping always clearly in mind that for the unmarried all voluntary expression of the sensitive appetite for venereal pleasure is contrary to reason and consequently immoral. A real esteem for the virtue of chastity plus a little common sense are sufficient to enable a sincere couple to maintain their balance in this regard.

The realization of rational order in marital sexuality requires adherence to the following general norms: Because the marriage contract confers equal rights and obligations upon the spouses either may desire marital union for the purpose of showing love, procuring children, strengthening unity, or physical release. As a human act between spouses who have become "two in one flesh," it should always be an act of mutual affection for it represents by its very nature the communion of husband and wife in the joy of procreating love. In the conjugal act partners make a mutually complementary gift of self at the physical, psychological, and spiritual levels of their being.

Hence, the act loses its profound significance if it is performed to secure purely selfish, individual satisfaction or if one partner refuses reasonable co-operation. Likewise the act loses its significance if the mutual gift is restricted by placing a direct obstacle to hinder its natural procreative process. Such a contraceptive obstacle would deprive the mutual gift of its life-giving, procreative character, thus rendering the conjugal act essentially meaningless because it would no longer represent an act by which the spouses mutually complete each other through giving freely and unreservedly what they are able.

It follows that, although the couple need not directly intend procreation in performing the marital act, they must always respect the natural physiological process of the act that they have freely performed. The reason that they need not directly intend procreation is that the act has other purposes in marriage. According to Catholic teaching, the marital act is subordinate to the primary purpose of marriage—the procreation and education of children. The fulfillment of this purpose requires the establishment of a society characterized by stability, love, intimacy, and so forth. In this situation, besides providing for procreation, conjugal relations become a normal means for fostering love, unity, and mutual support.

Furthermore, because physical union is an objectively good act all those normal manifestations of affection, mutual stimulation, and so on preceding and following the act are good in themselves. However, individual likes and dislikes vary widely in this regard so that charity requires a sincere respect for the feelings of the partner. This consideration clearly underlines the social aspect of the act. It always involves two persons, and any attempt to make it a source of purely personal gratification rather than a manifestation of mutual love destroys its meaning.

Finally, the marriage contract involves mutual obligations in this matter; that is, a spouse may not habitually refuse a *reasonable* request for conjugal relations. Such failure to co-operate would constitute a serious dereliction of duty. How-ever, if a husband refuses to support his family, if he has been drinking heavily, and so forth his request cannot be judged reasonable. At the same time charity and justice require sincere consideration for the partner during periods of ill health, un-usual fatigue, pregnancy, and so on. Partners should learn early in marriage how to communicate frankly on this important obligation lest even reasonable refusal be interpreted as selfish-ness or loss of affection.

Perhaps no practical application of Catholic moral principles has occasioned greater misunderstanding and disagreement than the Church's position on contraceptive birth control. The majority of organized non-Catholic religious groups have gone on record as not opposed to the practice when the family situa-tion seems to require it, while research indicates that it is no longer considered a moral issue by most non-Catholic American adults. Their attitude seems to be fairly well summarized in the statement unanimously adopted by one of the Protestant groups in 1954: "So long as it causes no harm to those involved, either immediately or over an extended period, none of the methods for controlling the number and spacing of the births of children has any special moral merit or demerit. It is the spirit in which the means is used, rather than whether it is 'natural' or 'artificial,' which defines its 'rightness' or 'wrong-ness.'"

We have cited this interesting statement because it points up clearly both disagreement with and misunderstanding of the Catholic position. According to this statement the morality of the practice is to be judged on the basis of the intention (spirit) with which it is used. Catholic doctrine maintains that three elements must be taken into consideration in judging the moral character of any human action: the objective nature of the action considered in itself; the personal reasons for performing it, or the motives; and the surrounding situation, or the circumstances. A defect in any of these elements vitiates the moral goodness of the action. For example, it is wrong to lie (an inherently evil act) even for a good motive; to give alms out of pride (a bad motive); to have marital relations in public (improper circumstances). As we shall point out, Catholics regard the use of contraceptives as an objectively defective moral act so that even when they are used with the right motives (spirit), the action remains immoral.

Moreover, the inference that the Catholic position is based on a distinction between *natural* and *artificial* means suggests that the basis for the Church's opposition to the practice is misunderstood. To be sure, these two terms are frequently used loosely in discussion, but Catholics are not opposed to the use of contraceptives *because* they are artificial or man-made, for Catholics make use of a great variety of "artificial" products each day. Hence, as used in this context, the term *natural* signifies that the means employed is in conformity with the nature and purpose of the conjugal act, whereas the term *artificial* implies that the means used is not in conformity, whether the hindrance results from an artifact, such as a condom, or from a "natural" act, such as premature withdrawal.

However, we would have to treat the Church's position on birth control in some detail even if it were not a source of disagreement and misunderstanding among non-Catholics. It appears that some Catholics regard it as little more than an ecclesiastical disciplinary measure consequently subject to reformulation, while others simply fail to follow it for a variety of reasons. A few studies, though based on relatively small, select numbers, give some indication that this latter group may be considerable.

Even before World War II, population studies showed that although the Catholic birth rate was higher than that of others in all comparable categories, the fertility of both Catholic and

Protestant couples tended to react to similar environments in the same direction. Likewise, in a representative, nationwide study of religious beliefs conducted for the *Catholic Digest* in 1952, it was found that only 51 per cent of those who expressed their religious preference as Catholic agreed with the Church's teaching on the use of contraceptives. When interpreting this statistic, however, it should be noted that roughly one third of those who expressed a preference for Catholicism did not attend mass regularly. The study did not reveal whether there was a relationship between church attendance and attitudes toward contraceptives.

In order to discuss the morality of birth control we must first define our terms and state our premises clearly. Failure to do this in the past has led to increased confusion rather than understanding. There can be no meeting of minds when we are talking about different things or basing our arguments on different premises of values. The broad terms *birth control* or *planned parenthood* have many meanings, including the planned limitation of family size through virtuous continence and the control of fertility through the immoral use of contraceptive devices or similar measures. In the following discussion we shall use the term *birth control* to cover all deliberate acts that are aimed directly at the antecedent frustration or hindrance of the fecundity of the conjugal act. It should be noted that birth control may be considered under various aspects: as a social act in its effects on the quality and growth of population, as a psychophysical act in its effects on marital satisfaction and happiness, and as a moral act in its effects on the development and perfection of the human person. Only this latter aspect is pertinent to our present treatment.

An intelligent judgment concerning the morality of birth control must be based on the logical application of general moral principles to this specific human act. It follows that people who base their considerations in this matter upon different moral principles will necessarily reach different conclusions.

This obvious point is all too frequently forgotten in current controversy. For example, the Christian who believes that the human person is a unity of body and soul, endowed with faculties of intellect and will and possessing an essential relationship of origin, dependence, and destiny to his Creator, will judge the morality of birth control differently from a materialist who maintains that man is only a highly developed animal. Unfortunately, many who do not accept the materialist's philosophy of life accept his conclusions in this matter because they have not made clear the implicit moral principles upon which their judgment is necessarily based. Thus, they continue to pay lip service to one set of moral principles while founding their conduct upon another.

The Catholic judgment on the morality of birth control implies the following premises: Men and women are created by God, stand in a relationship of essential dependence upon Him, and are destined to eternal happiness with Him in heaven. At the same time, the order of reason requires that things be used according to the purpose God intended in creating them. Men discover this purpose by studying the normal and essential operations of things. It follows that men act reasonably when they use for their self-development and perfection in God's service all those things which He has placed under their dominion. God alone is the Author and source of life. He has not placed life or the principles of life (sperm and ovum) under the creature's absolute dominion. Men hold these in trust from God, so that they must respect their own lives and that of others, and they may not destroy them for their own personal satisfaction.

Likewise, they must respect the natural process of the generative act in which they furnish the co-principles of life; that is, they may not place a direct, antecedent obstacle to hinder the natural physiological process of the reproductive act in which they have freely chosen to use faculties involving the co-principles of life. In other words, the function of sex (the possession and use of faculties involving the co-principles of life) has been entrusted to men and women for the good of the species, and right reason demands that it be employed accordingly. The sexual act has specific, highly unique qualities. It is the act designed for the propagation of the human race by the Creator himself, and its fruitful exercise requires the special co-operation of God, the Author of each new life.

In the light of these principles let us consider the morality of birth control. A study of the structure and function of the generative system indicates that its primary purpose is reproduction. The production of sperm in the male and the process of the menstrual cycle in woman are clearly geared to reproduction. Further, a study of the conjugal act indicates clearly that its primary purpose is to bring about the union of the co-principles of reproduction, sperm and ovum. Conception may not always follow the sexual act, but the act itself is designed to make the fusion of sperm and ovum possible. Although the immediate, experienced result of sexual relations is physical release, a temporary cessation of sexual desire, and an intimate, psychological union of the partners, these are consequent, accompanying effects of the act and clearly not the primary purpose either of the reproductive system or of sexual union.

Since marital union is an act by which husband and wife mutually complete each other by supplying that which the other lacks in terms of reproduction, its very meaning implies that each gives freely and unreservedly what they are able. It is precisely this generous, mutual gift of self that unites husband and wife in a procreating act of love. To deprive this mutual gift of its life-giving, generative character by placing a direct obstacle to the natural procreative process inherent in it, is to destroy the essential significance of the act. In other words, when a couple employ contraceptives they perform an act that is generative by its nature, but at the same time they attempt to frustrate or hinder its inherent reproductive purpose by deliberately placing an obstacle to the natural generative process. Hence, they are not acting as reasonable persons because they will and do not will the generative act at the same time. Such action constitutes a clear contradiction in the practical order, for the couple freely choose to perform a generative act, and at the same time they do not choose it, inasmuch as they attempt to frustrate its primary generative character.

This violation of the order of right reason in sexuality makes birth control a gravely immoral act. There are several factors involved in its gravity. It represents a serious deviation from an essential and necessary order in creation. The sexual act is the means that the Creator has ordained for the propagation of the race. If men and women wish to make use of their generative faculties, as reasonable beings they must follow the divine plan in doing so; that is, they must respect the inherent purpose of the act.

Moreover, the conjugal act has special significance because it deals with life. In using their reproductive faculties husband and wife supply the human co-principles of life and have the privilege of co-operating with the Creator in the production of new life. This power has been entrusted to them by God; in using it they must respect its sublime character. This means that they may not directly interfere with the natural relationship between physical union and procreation which exists in the total physiological process.

To summarize then, the moral evil of birth control consists in the positive and direct intervention in the process of procreation which the couple have freely initiated by their marital union. It should be noted that the essential evil of the act is not that it may hinder a possible conception. The union of the sperm and the ovum may or may not follow the conjugal act and is quite independent of the will of the spouses. The evil of birth control consists primarily in deviation from the order of right reason. By interfering with the natural process of the reproductive act, the spouses assume a dominion that they do not possess over their generative faculties.

Some people argue that spouses have the right to use birth control because the marital act has other purposes besides reproduction. Marital union does have other purposes which amply justify its use, but these purposes must not be achieved by means of an immoral act. Moral rectitude requires that the couple follow the order of right reason in their actions. If they desire to perform the conjugal act for any number of valid reasons they must respect the natural procreative process inherent in the act. It is not in their power to decide whether conception will follow from their union. They act in accord with right reason as long as they do not attempt to interfere with the natural physiological process that they have initiated in seeking marital relations. Thus, husband and wife do not act contrary to the order of reason if they desire sexual relations even when they are certain that conception cannot follow. In doing so they are seeking some of the other purposes that marital union achieves, while they are not interfering with the natural procreative process of the sexual act itself.

The Catholic viewpoint on birth control has been clearly stated by Pius XI in his encyclical *On Christian Marriage:* "Any use whatsoever of matrimony exercised in such a way that the act is deliberately frustrated in its natural power to generate life is an offense against the law of God and of nature, and those who indulge in such are branded with the guilt of grave sin." He shows that birth control violates the order of reason and is gravely sinful as follows: "Since, therefore, the conjugal act is destined primarily by nature for the begetting of children, those who in exercising it deliberately frustrate its natural power and purpose, sin against nature and commit a deed which is shameful and intrinsically evil."

Finally, it should be noted that the Catholic position on this matter does not represent a mere disciplinary regulation promulgated for the direction of the faithful and consequently binding only them. Rather, it is an obvious application of general moral principles to a specific act binding all who possess the use of reason. It follows that neither the Pope nor any one else has the power to change it. When Catholics say that the use of birth control is *unnatural* or *against nature*, they mean it is contrary to the created order of things which right reason can discover and to which reasonable creatures must adhere in their actions. The rejection of the Catholic viewpoint in this matter implies either a lack of logic in reasoning or a denial of the basic moral principles upon which it is based.

Considering the widespread contemporary demand for some type of planned parenthood, it may appear rather paradoxical that the problem of infertility has likewise received increasing attention during recent years. The desire for children appears universal among normal couples. Most young people who enter marriage anticipate having some children sooner or later. If their union proves to be sterile they are bound to be seriously disappointed, not a little humiliated, and rather sensitive to adverse public opinion. Since it is estimated that perhaps one out of every ten marriages is involuntarily sterile, medical scientists have sought various means to remedy the situation.

Although the couple's desire to have children is morally good and the physician's consequent efforts to help them are worthy of praise, the means employed to remedy infertility must conform to right moral principles. In this connection the process called artificial insemination perhaps raises the most questions at the present time. Broadly speaking, artificial insemination refers to any process in which artificial or extrinsic means are used to assist the semen in effecting impregnation.

The first moral issue to be decided involves the source of the semen. Modern medical science has discovered that in some cases it is possible to effect impregnation of the wife by using semen contributed by some one other than her husband. This is called donor insemination. It should be obvious that this process is immoral and constitutes a grave sin. The marriage contract confers mutual rights and obligations upon the partners which they must exercise personally and cannot delegate to a third party.

In this connection it is well to note that the marriage contract does not confer the right to *parenthood* but the mutual, exclusive, and perpetual right to *acts* that are of their very nature proper for begetting children. The use of donor insemination represents a type of adultery. The civil courts of the United

States have not yet ruled directly on the legality of such insemination, though there are indications that it would be regarded as adultery. According to French and English law a wife who becomes artificially inseminated in this manner is judged guilty of adultery.

What moral issues are involved if the semen of the husband is used in the process? Obviously, the means employed to obtain the semen must conform to the moral law. Hence, semen may not be obtained by masturbation, withdrawal during intercourse, the use of the condom, rectal massage of the prostate and the seminal vesicles, or puncture of the testicles. Furthermore, any process by which semen is first procured from the husband and later used for artificial insemination is judged illicit because the conjugal act is by its very nature a personal act of co-operation. It is only this natural act that husband and wife give each other the right to perform when they enter marriage.

Are any forms of artificial insemination morally licit? If we take the broad definition of the term—namely, that artificial insemination refers to any process in which artificial or extrinsic means are used to assist the semen in effecting impregnation—then there are two possibilities. It is judged morally licit to collect by means of a syringe the semen deposited in the wife's vagina in normal intercourse and to eject this semen into the external os, cervical canal, or uterus in order to provide a better chance for impregnation. Also, it is morally licit to insert a cervical spoon or similar instrument into the vagina before intercourse in order to facilitate the passage of the sperm into the womb. These two methods are the only morally licit means of assisting insemination thus far discovered by medical science.

Another point of conjugal morality giving rise to considerable discussion during recent years is the practice of periodic continence based on the rhythm method. Stated briefly, the couple profit by their knowledge of the alternating phases of sterility and fecundity in the menstrual cycle and deliberately restrict marital relations to a definite period in the cycle in order to avoid or promote pregnancy. We are not interested here in the physiological assumptions upon which this practice is based, but a discussion of the moral principles involved in its licit use is pertinent and will serve further to clarify the Catholic position on birth control.

To judge the morality of practicing periodic continence we must consider whether it is a morally permissible means considered in itself and under what circumstances its use is morally licit. Considered in itself, the practice of rhythm does not constitute a deviation from right order or the moral law. The couple engage in normal marital relations and respect the natural physiological conditions of the reproductive process that they have initiated. Contrary to birth control, the practice of rhythm does not interfere with the normal physiological process freely set in motion by the act of intercourse. Hence, in itself it must be judged a morally indifferent means and, like all such means, becomes morally good or evil in use according to the conditions under which it is practiced.

Under what conditions is the practice of periodic continence morally permissible? They can be summarized under three heads. In the first place, both partners must freely agree to the practice. The marriage contract confers the mutual right to marital relations and the reciprocal mutual obligation to grant the reasonable request for the use of that right, so that neither spouse may restrict the other's use of this right without consent. Further, the couple must be capable of bearing the tension and restraint the practice may involve. Thus, it would become illicit if it seriously threatened the couple's growth in mutual love and unity, or if it placed them in the proximate occasion of violating chastity.

Last, there must be sufficient reason for its practice. Since it serves as a means to achieve an end its use will be morally good or evil to the extent that the reason or purpose for which it is practiced is morally good or evil. This purpose must be judged in terms of the total obligations that the couple have assumed in their state in life. Briefly, if they choose to make use of their marital rights, their life vocation requires that they seek mutual development and perfection in the service of God by co-operating with the Creator in the procreation and education of children. It follows that a couple may make use of periodic continence to improve their chances to procreate, always provided that the first two conditions mentioned above are fulfilled. When may they use it for the purpose of avoiding or postponing pregnancy?

Before answering this question we had best clarify several points of Catholic teaching frequently misunderstood. Marriage partners are free not to use their marital rights provided that they do so for unselfish reasons, that is, in order to free themselves for the more complete service of God and their fellow men. Couples who are sterile either temporarily or permanently may licitly use their marital rights. The conjugal act fulfills several purposes, and as long as its use is subordinated to the primary purpose of marriage, it is licit. Periodic continence based on the rhythm method is not merely tolerated by the Church on the grounds that it is a highly unreliable method for avoiding pregnancy. Couples who employ it have the deliberate intention of avoiding conception, and it is the moral rectitude of their intention which is at issue.

In his address to the Italian Catholic Union of Midwives (October 29, 1951), commonly called the "Apostolate of the Midwife," Pius XII summarizes Catholic teaching on the licitness of using periodic continence. First, he points out the positive obligation to procreate. "Matrimony obliges to a state of life which, while carrying with it certain rights, also imposes the fulfillment of a positive work connected with that state of life." This positive work is to provide for the conservation of the human race. Next, he calls attention to the general principle that applies to the non-fulfillment of an obligation. "In this case we can apply the general principle that a positive contribution may be withheld if serious reasons, independent of the good will of the persons obliged to make it, show that such contribution is inopportune, or prove that the claimant—in this case the human race—cannot in equity require it."

When we apply this general principle to the use of periodic continence, we conclude that marriage partners may practice it if their personal condition or external circumstances are such that childbearing and child rearing in their case can be reasonably judged inopportune, or if their condition or external circumstances are such that the human race cannot in equity demand that they fulfill their obligation to provide for its conservation. The obligation remains, but special conditions or circumstances render its fulfillment either inopportune or unreasonable. Because these conditions or circumstances may persist for a time or throughout the duration of marriage, the practice may be licit for a time or throughout the entire duration of marriage. In either case, since the obligation is serious the judgment that it need not be fulfilled must be based on serious reasons.

Finally, the Pope lists several general categories of conditions or circumstances that may provide these serious reasons. "From the obligation of making this positive contribution it is possible to be exempt, for a long time and even for the whole duration of married life, if there are serious reasons, such as those provided in the so-called 'indications' of the medical, eugenical, economic, and social order. It therefore follows that the observance of the infertile periods may be licit from the moral point of view; and under the conditions mentioned it is so in fact."

Thus, the Pope tells us that conditions or circumstances of a medical, eugenical, economic, and social nature may exist which are signs that a couple will encounter serious difficulty in carrying out their procreative function or which point to family limitation as a remedy. On the basis of these "indications" the couple must judge prudently whether or not the positive fulfillment of their obligations can be considered inopportune or whether the demand to fulfill it can reasonably be made. At present the practice of periodic continence tends to become a moral issue not primarily as a means of absolutely excluding children but as a means of postponing or spacing their arrival. The current birth rate indicates that the majority of couples enter marriage with the intention of rearing families. Because of special problems, however, some of them desire to use the practice for the purpose of either postponing or spacing their pregnancies. Inasmuch as they do not intend to avoid the obligations of their marriage vocation, this will be licit provided all the moral implications of the practice are considered.

By way of summary, the following general rules concerning the use of periodic continence may be formulated. Both husband and wife must freely agree to its use. They must be reasonably capable of practicing it. They must have serious reasons for using it throughout the childbearing period. Under special circumstances they may use it for postponing pregnancy at the beginning of marriage, but prudence requires that they have sound reasons for doing so. They may use it for prudently spacing births more equally throughout the childbearing period.[1]

The morality of sterilization is pertinent to the present discussion because it is now promoted as a method of birth control. In former times it was recommended primarily to control reproduction among the so-called mental defectives and criminals. Many states have such immoral laws although their ineffectiveness in reducing the number of mentally defective persons in the population has caused them to fall into disuse in some instances. Today sterilization is being advocated as a superior, highly "safe" method of birth control or, as the popular literature puts it, as "a permanent protection against parent-

[1] Cf. John L. Thomas, S.J., *Marriage and Rhythm* (The Newman Press, Westminster, Md., 1957), for a more complete treatment of this whole subject.

hood." In addition to the clinics established for this purpose, there is some evidence to suggest that it is also employed by a considerable number of surgeons as a routine procedure when they judge a future pregnancy would be harmful to the health of their patients.

When used for this purpose sterilization of the female consists in tying or crushing the tubes that normally serve as a passageway for the ripened ovum from the ovary to the uterus. This operation is termed a *salpingectomy*. An alternate method in use includes cauterizing the tubes by inserting an electric wire through the uterus. Sterilization in the male consists in tying the tubes that conduct the sperm from the testicles to the urethra, or the tube from which they are ejaculated in the sexual act. This operation is called a vasectomy.

Sterilization whether in men or women constitutes a mutilation of the sexual organs and consequently frustrates the natural generative purpose of these faculties. When used for either eugenic or birth control purposes such direct sterilization is a gravely immoral act. Man's dominion over the members of his body is limited to using them according to their natural purposes as the order of right reason directs him. He does not have the power to destroy or mutilate them in order to frustrate the natural purposes they were designed to fulfill. Whether the state or the individual attempts to do this, either usurps a dominion which neither possesses.

In an address on the moral problems of married life (October 29, 1951) Pius XII clearly stated the Church's position on this point. "Direct sterilization—that is, the sterilization which aims, either as a means or as an end in itself, to render childbearing impossible—is a grave violation of the moral law, and therefore unlawful. Even public authority has no right, whatever 'indication' it may use as an excuse, to permit it, and much less to prescribe it or use it to the detriment of innocent human beings."[2]

[2] Indirect sterilization—that is, sterilization that results from an operation performed to remove or alleviate a pathological condition in the generative faculties—is permissible but need not be discussed in detail here.

Finally, there is evidence to suggest that a new type of sterilization may become possible by the use of drugs taken orally. One of these (phosphorylated hesperidin) presently receiving some publicity is clearly an anti-fertility pill, that is, a contraceptive measure taken to assure direct temporary sterilization. As such its use is obviously immoral. Other drugs that attempt to regulate the menstrual cycle by stopping ovulation may likewise result in assuring direct temporary sterility and their use for this purpose is clearly immoral. On the other hand, if such drugs should be found definitely useful in treating pathological conditions of the reproductive system, their use under such circumstances would constitute indirect sterilization and would consequently be morally permissible provided such treatment was directly achieved and primarily intended.

The Catholic position on the morality of abortion is perhaps more openly rejected today than at any previous time in the Christian past. The practice of abortion is obviously related to family morals and consequently must be treated here, but our primary concern is to clarify a few misconceptions rather than to present an exhaustive treatment of the subject. Specifically, because of their opposition to so-called therapeutic abortions, Catholics are accused by the uninformed of callously sacrificing the life of the mother to save that of her unborn child. This timeworn, hoary accusation is still promulgated by promoters of birth control, and it has assumed almost the status of folklore in the popular non-Catholic mind.

What are the facts in the case? In the first place Catholics regard direct, induced abortion as murder. Hence, the estimated annual 500,000 to 1,000,000 criminal abortions, which the civil authorities seem little inclined to prevent, are considered so many unsolved murders by Catholics. Further, Catholics believe that "therapeutic" abortions constitute murder. By a therapeutic abortion we mean a direct abortion that is induced for the purpose of preserving the health of the mother. An abortion is direct when the sole immediate result of the procedure is the termination of pregnancy before viability; it is indirect when the abortion is the by-product of a procedure that is immediately directed to the cure of a pathological condition of the mother.

The Catholic position is based on the principle that human life is sacred and must be respected in the unborn as well as in others. Any operation that directly kills either the mother or the child is immoral. The life of each is inviolable, and we may not kill one to save the other. In the hypothetical case where the doctor might save the life of one by directly killing the other, Catholics maintain that he is dealing with two innocent people, each possessing an equal and clear title to life. Consequently he must make every effort to save both lives, but under no circumstances may he directly murder one in order to save the life of the other.

Right reason can dictate no other solution. However, since opposition to the Catholic position persists in some quarters, it may be well to note what competent medical authorities think of the need for therapeutic abortions. Speaking to a recent Congress of the American College of Surgeons, Doctor Roy J. Heffernan declared: "Anyone who performs a therapeutic abortion is either ignorant of modern medical methods of treating the complications of pregnancy or is unwilling to take the time to use them." His view is corroborated by medical investigations both in the United States and abroad. Moreover, statistics show that maternal mortality rates in Catholic hospitals are as low, and in many cases lower, than in hospitals where therapeutic abortion is not considered a moral issue.

Up to this point we have been discussing direct abortions. It may be well to add a few words concerning indirect abortions. As we stated, an abortion is judged to be indirect when the interruption of the pregnancy is the undesired effect of a procedure that is immediately directed to secure some other good purpose such as the stopping of a hemorrhage or the removal of a cancer. If a sufficiently serious reason exists—that is, if the procedure is really judged necessary to save the life of the mother, and the abortion is indirect as defined above—it is morally licit.

Starting primarily with the Renaissance and the Reformation, disagreement with the Catholic position on the value of virginity has been consistent and widespread. Although the comparison between the state of marriage and virginity permeates Christian ascetical writing it appears to be singularly fruitful in generating exaggeration and misunderstanding among Catholics and non-Catholics alike. Even in the early Christian centuries heretics like Marcion, who claimed that in praising virginity the Christians condemned marriage, had to be refuted by the Church Fathers. Luther and Calvin popularized this charge in their day, and it still remains an unquestioned assumption among many at present. The official position of the Church was stated in the 24th Session of the Council of Trent: "the married state is not to be preferred to the state of virginity or celibacy," and further, "it is better and happier to remain in virginity or celibacy than to be joined in matrimony."

This doctrine is based on the traditional distinction between the precepts and the counsels stated in the Gospels. All Christians are bound to follow Christ in the way of the precepts, but some are invited to follow Him in the more perfect way of the counsels. "'If thou wilt be perfect, go sell what thou hast . . . and come, follow me'" (Matt. 19:21) and, "'Not all can accept this teaching; but those to whom it has been given. . . . and there are eunuchs who have made themselves so for the sake of the kingdom of heaven. Let him accept it who can'" (Matt. 19:11–12). Those who heed this invitation aspire to a following of Christ which is more perfect than that required by the precepts. By devoting themselves to prayer, sacrifice, and the apostolate they strive to forget themselves in complete dedication to the service of God and neighbor. God does not impose this renunciation of self on all Christians; it is offered as a free choice, an invitation to imitate Christ more perfectly.

Catholic teaching on the value of virginity should cause no difficulty for the intelligent Christian. Inasmuch as man is created to serve God and this service admits of different degrees of completeness, it should be evident that the state of life that permits the most complete dedication to God's service will be ranked highest and most perfect. This preference for virginity involves a comparison between various states of life, not between individuals in these states.

Furthermore, it does not represent a devaluation of the state of matrimony. Although marriage is a sacrament and, hence, a divinely planned vocation leading to perfection, the individual Christian is free to dedicate himself to a more exclusive service of God if he possesses the necessary qualifications. Catholics have a high esteem for the state of virginity not because sex is considered impure or evil, but because the voluntary abstinence from its use frees the individual for a more unrestricted service of God and for a more perfect imitation of Christ.

We shall conclude our treatment of marriage and morals with a brief consideration of the single life. This is pertinent because the beliefs people hold concerning sex and marriage will be reflected in their attitudes toward the single life. Societies that place great value on reproduction and in which the family is the major social vehicle for integrating the individual in the community make marriage a near necessity for all normal adults. On the other hand, in a complex, highly industrialized society like our own, little emphasis is placed on begetting heirs, while the social system makes it possible to satisfy many of the needs formerly fulfilled only by the family. Hence, marriage is not a strict necessity in our culture, but other factors operate to make it very popular. Primary among these are the needs for companionship, security, and intimate emotional support, which are rendered more imperative by a shift in emphasis from the large extended family system, capable of absorbing individual married couples and unmarried members, to the small nuclear type composed only of husband, wife, and immature offspring.

In this connection it should be noted that individuals in the religious state or in the priesthood have a recognized, socially structured life which clearly defines their relationships to others, while compensating for their lack of marriage partner and family by directing their energy and affection toward the formally dedicated service of God and His children. The position of the unmarried in society, however, is not so clearly defined. In every enduring culture, marriage is the key institution regulating most acceptable relationships between the sexes. Among adults the majority of these relationships tend to proceed on a couple basis. The minority who do not marry will necessarily be affected by all these factors both in their past conditioning and in their present social expectations. Moreover, because the unmarried remain potentially marriageable their status remains somewhat marginal and indeterminate. In contrast to married people and consecrated celibates, the social system makes little provision for them.

Are there many who lead a single life in modern society? Although Americans are the most married of all Western peoples, roughly one out of ten never takes the step. At the same time many more are living a single life either because of separation, divorce, or widowhood. Reasons for remaining single are varied, ranging from deliberate choice to various physical, psychic, and social factors. In general we tend to think of the special problems of singleness in terms of women. Modern wars and political upheavals have taken a heavy toll of men. Further, women in all Western societies do not enjoy the same opportunities as men in initiating the dating and courtship processes that normally lead to marriage. They are far from helpless in this regard of course, but the aggressive woman still tends to frighten off most masculine candidates for marriage. Like the young Juliet with her Romeo, most girls sense that society expects them to play a waiting game: "Or if thou think'st I am too quickly won, I'll frown and be perverse and say thee nay."

Unmarried men undoubtedly have their problems, but it is commonly assumed that they can solve them by settling down to marriage when they so choose. It is believed that this solution is not so readily available for women once they have passed the first fair blush of youth. Statistics tell us that at thirty they have a fifty-fifty chance of marrying, while at forty their chances are reduced to one out of six. These figures merely tell us what percentage of women do marry at these various stages. They give us no information concerning those who do not marry or their reasons for remaining single. We cannot assume that all women desire to marry, should marry, or would be happier if married. Likewise, it is unrealistic to deny that there are many singletons who would now like to marry provided they met a suitable mate.

What is the Catholic viewpoint concerning the single state? Catholics maintain that all persons capable (physically, juridically, and so forth) of marriage have the right to marry. Although the human group as such has an obligation to propagate itself no specific individual is bound by this obligation, so that he may choose not to enter marriage provided he does so for morally licit motives. In comparing states of life, Catholics place consecrated virginity highest, then dedicated widowhood, then marriage, then the unmarried or single state. This is a comparison of states of life, that is, of various ways of imitating Christ; it is not a comparison between individuals within these various states of life. All of these states can lead to perfection, and the Church has canonized members from each category. In other words, Catholics maintain that although all are bound to follow Christ, either through choice or chance they may do so in various ways.

Thus for the single woman, as for all mankind, essential fulfillment consists in developing one's capacities and potentialities in the service of God. In the Christian outlook on life, this is the heart of the matter: How can I best serve God in my circumstances and thus realize my true purpose in life? Whether singleness be deliberately chosen or the result of other factors, personal or social, the first requisite for success is the full acceptance of it and what it personally and socially entails. The single woman must realize that her primary purpose in life remains unchanged; she differs from her sisters in the means available to achieve this purpose.

In practice, full acceptance means that she will reject the "escapes" sometimes used by others. She will not attempt to console herself by pointing out that some married people or religious are miserable and unhappy in their vocation. She will not feel insecure and retreat from life as if she had "missed the boat." Further, she must realize that she remains a social being. This is relatively easy for her married or religious sisters because their vocations by their very nature tend to draw them out of themselves. The singleton must cultivate warm friendships, and since society tends to restrict these with men, she should maintain close ties with other girls, her married friends, and the members of her own family. Like all people, she needs to feel needed. She can achieve this by doing her work well and, if it does not allow full expression for her creativity, by contributing time and effort to other activities.

Finally, the single woman must dedicate herself to goals that transcend the self. She faces the problem of self-centeredness perhaps more than others. Hence, the concept of mutual service in the Christian community assumes key importance for her. To serve Christ in His members, by example and cooperation at work, by the numberless opportunities for sympathy, kindness, and love available in contacts with others, by engaging in some of the varied forms of Catholic action, by rendering witness to Christ through her balanced development, attitudes, and efforts in her career—all these means are at hand provided they are recognized and used.

These general directives merely spell out the requisite conditions for all mature living. More specifically, the single woman should regard her vocation as a special invitation to sanctity. As St. Paul reminds us, she is freed from many of the consuming concerns of her married sisters and consequently can give herself more fully to God. Like everyone else she will face problems in life. Some derive from the social system; others from her state of singleness. Nothing is to be gained by condemning society or rejecting her femininity. She will find her fulfillment only by clearly understanding her essential purpose in life, by taking active steps to realize her human capacities, and by dedicating herself in a practical way to the service of Christ in His members. This is the basic principle of all Christian living. Those who "walk alone" must, perchance, use more resourcefulness in applying it.

CHAPTER VI

American Society

Our description of the Catholic viewpoint on sex and marriage contained in the last two chapters indicates that Catholics have a concise, clearly defined, and well-integrated set of values, standards, and practical norms to guide their attitudes and conduct in these areas. As a result Catholics constitute not only an identifiable religious minority but a distinct subculture. This is to say that they cherish a family system based on a philosophy of life differing in many significant respects from that currently supported in American society. Under these circumstances they can attempt to maintain their family system either by isolating themselves from the influence of the dominant culture or by limited integration.

Complete isolation is not easily achieved in modern society, although a few small groups such as some of the Mennonites in the United States and the Dukhobors in Canada appear to have had considerable success. Many national and racial minorities maintained—or endured—practical isolation during their early years in America. As we pointed out in Chapter II, some ethnic groups of the Catholic minority established strong solidarity around their national parishes and constructed cultural "fences" to hedge their members off from outside influences. These definitely served to slow down the process of integration, but at best they could only partially shield group members from the effects of social change taking place in the society around them. At the present time descendants of the "old" immigration have ceased to be identifiable as national minorities, while the descendants of the "new" are rapidly following their lead in moving toward limited integration.

By limited integration we mean that the members of a minority group mix freely in society and follow the generally accepted social goals and patterns of conduct except when these openly conflict with the realization of their moral system. This is roughly the position of the majority of Catholics in American society today. For better or for worse, the Catholic minority is being gradually assimilated, so that Catholic families as a whole are subjected to the same influences and pressures as are all other families in American society.

This raises the question of the special problems they will encounter in trying to maintain their family system intact. The rapid transformation of America from a rural to an industrialized urban society set the stage for manifold changes in the traditional family structure. The statuses and roles of husband and wife, of parents and children, of the married couple and their extended family must necessarily be modified by the adjustments required to meet the changed situation. Catholic families, like all others, must adapt to reality if they would survive, but they differ from other families to the extent that they must work out their adjustments in terms of their own distinctive ideals and standards. They may not simply follow the solutions worked out by those in the dominant culture because these solutions may be based on different premises of values. As members of a religious minority holding distinct views regarding sex and marriage they must evaluate new patterns of conduct in terms of their own standards.

Unfortunately Catholics and non-Catholics alike have been forced to adjust to such widespread and frequent change both in society at large and in their immediate families that they remain somewhat confused concerning what has happened. They recognize that numerous changes have occurred in family patterns even within the short span of their own experience (parents with growing adolescents are reminded of this daily) yet they find it difficult to judge their significance because everything in society seems to be undergoing change at the same time. For this reason we feel that the best approach to understanding the special problems of the Catholic minority will be to describe how the present state of confusion on the family front has developed and to point out the major pertinent areas of confusion in contemporary society.

Theoretically the shift from a rural to an industrialized urban environment occurring during the past seventy-five years in America could have taken place within the broad framework of traditional values related to sex and marriage. This is to say that basic family standards could have been preserved although the social means implementing them would have been modified to meet new situations. As a matter of historical fact this did not occur, because subtle changes had been going on in the minds of Americans concerning their traditional beliefs. When they were required to formulate new patterns of conduct in their changing environment, it soon became apparent that they no longer agreed on a set of doctrines concerning the nature and purpose of man and of society. Traditional family ideals and standards were consequently deprived of their foundation; they were, so to speak, left suspended, lacking a common point of departure in an agreed system of values. It should not come as a surprise, therefore, to learn that today they are widely regarded as "relative," wholly subject to change together with the rest of the social system.

This superficial view is prevalent because much that has passed as social science is mere description rather than analysis. Many scientists are reluctant to acknowledge the pertinence of values for understanding a social system. Alva Myrdal called attention to this trait in the opening chapter of her *Nation and Family:* "An established tendency to drive values underground, to make the analysis appear scientific by omitting certain basic assumptions from the discussion, has too often emasculated the social sciences as agencies for rationality in social and political life." Because they accept uncritically an inadequate definition of what is scientific many social scientists lose sight of the obvious principle that "to be truly rational, a social program, like a practical judgment, is a conclusion based upon premises of values as well as upon facts."

Hence, both the significance and the extent of failure to agree on traditional values pass unperceived in our society. Yet, as Montesquieu pointed out long ago, the beginning of a nation's decadence dates from the time it loses sight of the principles upon which it was founded. The implicit and explicit rejection of these principles has proceeded far and from varied sources in America. For example, among many political scientists the idea of an objective moral order and natural rights has been old hat for half a century, though Jefferson's justly famous preamble to the Declaration of Independence states that all men are created equal, that they are endowed by their Creator with certain inalienable rights, and that the purpose of government is to secure these rights.

Likewise, many cultural anthropologists, who enjoy such popularity today as we move into the one-world concept, assure us that other cultures and ethics are equally valid. All ethical systems are relative. There are no objective, unchanging concepts of "right" and "wrong" by which they can be judged. In education we have by-passed what was sound in Dewey and moved toward a theory of group participation in which the primary goal is to teach students "social integration," "group harmony," or "interpersonal relations." This teaching of "how to belong to a group," built up of eclectic borrowings from the social sciences, psychology, and group dynamics, has no place for the idea that the individual is personally accountable for his conduct and should be trained accordingly. Indeed, because the public schools in a pluralistic society can teach nothing concerning the ultimate end of man, the laws of moral conduct, the reasons why there are good and evil or why there are virtues and vices, educators are reduced to promoting "permissive" attitudes toward all systems of values, though the end result continues to be the production of ethical eunuchs.

In the behavioral disciplines, sociologists shift emphasis from one form of social determinism to another, psychologists keep reformulating various species of stimulus-reaction determinism, and psychiatrists proceed as if they are dealing with the mechanisms of blind internal urges rather than with rational beings. There can be no question of an objective moral order and personal responsibility to God in this context. Values, norms, and conduct are all relative. The key words become *adjustment* and *adaptation*. Why adjust? Obviously to avoid tension and frustration. Adapt to what? To the group, for only by "community-centered cohesion" can "social tensions" be reduced and "equilibrium" be achieved.

This concept of equilibrium is based on a rather crude mechanistic theory of personality development. The human person is considered nothing more than a bundle of blind urges or drives, variously channeled through past experience and constantly seeking expression or satisfaction in contact with the external world. The secret of mature personality development, therefore, is not restraint or self-control (for these urges will out!); rather, it consists in patterning their expression in terms of group expectations. It follows that traditional Christianity, with its doctrine of self-denial and repression, is harmful and must give way before the findings of "science." In this context, *guilt* has become a dirty word, personal responsibility a comfortable illusion, and religion a convenient instrument for securing group harmony or "harmonious integration."

Out of this background has developed a theory of "communications" in the practical order which implies that all disagreements and conflicts result either from failure to understand each other's language (semantics) or from "blocks" in the channels of communication. Thus disagreements between nations, between management and worker, between diverse systems of morality, and so forth can all be settled without conflict if we would only have the patience to sit down together and "talk out" our differences. Evidently the belief that parties in opposition may understand each other only too well, that they may actually seek to achieve conflicting goals because they embrace different value systems can only be the product of an "authoritarian" mind, than which there is nothing judged more disreputable in a pluralistic society. Used in this context, pluralistic is a weasel word signifying that really mature citizens will maintain an open (permissive) mind; that is, they will recognize no absolutes—values, norms, and patterns of conduct are all to be considered relative.

It bears repeating that the norms regulating the conduct of men, as well as the institutional objectives that they establish as goals in the political, economic, and social order, receive their basic meaning and sanction from the conception of human nature that men hold. In the final analysis confusion and conflict in practice can be reduced to divergence in value premises. It is because modern men no longer agree on sex and marriage values that they disagree on social practices associated with them. Through a strange lack of logic the majority of Americans still respect traditional Christian family standards in theory, while their scientific disciplines reject or ignore the premises upon which these standards are logically based, and their approved norms of daily conduct imply other values. Thus, they fail to see the implicit contradiction in promoting or tolerating patterns of conduct that render the achievement of these standards highly improbable if not practically impossible.

Such persons find themselves caught in a serious dilemma. On the one hand they maintain a specific set of ideals and values and strongly condemn their violation; on the other they tolerate or promote practices that render frequent violations almost inevitable. Now, when both traditional value and contradictory practice are strongly supported by popular sentiment, the result is really a latent "cultural discontinuity." By this we mean that the situation indicates the hidden conflict between contradictory aspects of two divergent value systems. Briefly, a family value is cherished without implementing the social means necessary for its practical achievement, while a set of opposing practices is adopted without clearly recognizing the premises on which they are logically based. In a rapidly changing pluralistic society like our own, these latent "cultural discontinuities" are frequently treated as "lags" or conflicts arising from failure to adjust. In reality they are much more significant than that for they imply a conflict of value systems that can be resolved only by a definite choice of one or the other.

To be sure, various organized religious groups in American society retain clearly defined views concerning human nature, the purpose of marriage, and moral rectitude in sexual behavior. However, inasmuch as they constitute minority groups, they are not in positions to control popular trends affecting sex and marriage. Indeed, research suggests that under circumstances of rapid change and pluralism the impulse to conform is so great that even members of these groups tend to "follow the crowd" in practice.

Several perceptive modern writers have uncovered the reflection of this tendency in the popular mind. David Riesman in *The Lonely Crowd* speaks of the shift from "inner-" to "outer-directedness." William H. Whyte describes it as the development of a "groupthink" mentality in which the buck-passing of a moral decision becomes in itself a moral act, for "who am I to differ from the group? and besides, the system attends to this so much better than I can." What Riesman and Whyte do not seem to understand is that "outer-directedness" and "moral buck-passing" are the only practical alternatives that remain for people once the norms governing their conduct have been divorced from an integrated value system based on a clearly defined view of man. Of course, if we accept the belief, implicit in most modern "scientific" approaches, that the human person is nothing more than a complex combination of basic urges, conditioned reflexes, and acquired habits striving to achieve "equilibrium" in a group composed of similarly constituted individuals, there remains no rational basis for "inner-directedness" or making moral decisions.

There are several reasons why we have thought it necessary to call attention to this aspect of pluralism in contemporary sex and marriage values. It is well to note that change may be reflected in the family system at the levels of ultimate values, family standards, or conduct. Problems arise when changes introduced at one level prove incompatible with accepted elements at the other two levels. For example, changes introduced at the level of conduct may conflict with accepted family standards and may be opposed to the traditional values upon which the family system was founded. Particularly under conditions of rapid change the failure to integrate conduct, family standards, and basic values leads to frustration and confusion, for the discrepancy between accepted ideals and daily practice then becomes personally experienced.

Much of the current malaise and confusion associated with the diversity in sex and marriage behavior stems from the difficulty of logically integrating pertinent values, norms, and conduct in a pluralistic society undergoing rapid change. When the social system is integrated these elements are logically and mutually supportive. When a system is characterized by pluralism members of society are presented with socially acceptable alternatives in each of these categories and are faced with the difficult task of developing their own integrated system.

It follows that tension and frustration resulting either from failure to integrate values, norms, and conduct or from conflict among opposing value systems may appear at various points in the American family system. For example, they may be manifested within individual family members themselves or within the domestic unit when husband and wife, parents and children embrace divergent ideals and standards. Likewise, individual married couples may have different values from those accepted by their relatives or by other families in the community. This can easily happen in a society characterized by rapid vertical and horizontal mobility. Further, family values of a minority group may be in conflict with those supported by society or by other minorities. Finally, a given set of family values may be in conflict with the values implied in other sub-systems, such as the economic, political, or social.

We have emphasized the pertinence of considering values when studying changes in our family system because in a society characterized by pluralism and rapid change there is a tendency to forget that basic values have social demands. As we have explained, these constitute the complex of social conditions, attitudes, and patterns of conduct that are logically related to the effective implementation of a value in a given society. Failure to take cognizance of these may readily produce frustration and conflict if individuals are encouraged by Church or parental training to embrace a specific set of values while thoughtlessly adopting new behavioral patterns that render their achievement improbable or overly difficult. These "built-in" contradictions may occur so frequently in our society because there is need for constant adjustment and adaptation, the long-range consequences of some adjustments are not readily perceived, and the average individual is not trained to think in terms of ultimate value premises and their application to new situations.

We can conclude from the analysis above that personal frustration and family disorganization could best be avoided in an integrated society. By an integrated society we mean a social system in which the members hold roughly the same set of basic values, define marriage ideals in the same way, and consequently organize their political, economic, social, and religious institutions so as to support or at least not to hinder the achievement of these ideals. In such a society clearly defined norms of conduct are gradually developed at the practical level, and group members respect those who live up to them. Young people are reared in terms of a definite sexual code, and couples entering marriage know what is expected of them as partners and parents. These expectancies constitute the framework within which personal development is meaningfully defined and the pursuit of happiness achieves significance. Whether a perfectly integrated society exists anywhere may be open to question; however, one point is clear: American society, particularly in regard to sex and marriage behavior, is not well integrated.

Thus far we have indicated the sources of pluralism, together with the personal and social conflicts that inevitably arise when integration is lacking. There remains to point out some of the pertinent areas most profoundly affected by pluralism. The purpose of the following discussion is to describe the general climate of opinion and the social situation within which members of the Catholic minority are reared, enter marriage, and establish their families. Teaching experience has taught us that the profound significance of religious minority status cannot be adequately appreciated without this knowledge.

Let us first consider confusion in the area related to sex. One of the most imperative drives every society must regulate among its members is that concerned with the reproduction of the species. The exercise of this function may be considered either a moral act—and consequently its regulation will fall under the general norms specifying the morality of all human acts —or merely an act implying more or less important social consequences—and hence its regulation will be governed by the assumed needs of the group. As followers of Western cultural traditions, most Americans theoretically adhere to the first type of regulation: the exercise of the reproductive function is a moral act, and stable, monogamous marriage is the social institution established to channel its legitimate use.

This theoretical position is widely belied in practice. Because the premises of values underlying practical programs of action are seldom made explicit, divergent patterns of conduct are tolerated with apparently slight awareness that they contradict traditional values. Time-honored standards and rules persist as cultural ideals, but as we have taken pains to point out, the concept of man giving them meaning and significance is openly rejected by some, conveniently ignored by others, and apparently judged not pertinent by many more.

Two practical consequences follow. In the first place, Americans can reach little practical agreement on the regulation of sex. When there is no consensus on premises of values, there can be none on practical programs of action. Open and blatant exploitation of the sexual drive, with obvious detrimental social consequences, is tolerated in advertising, entertainment, art, literature, and so forth. Moreover, the process by which one set of standards and patterns of conduct is strongly advocated in theory and a contradictory set is tolerated and promoted in practice gives rise to serious personal contradictions and tensions. As a result sex has come to preoccupy people's minds excessively, assuming a position out of all proportion to its importance in stable social life.

This current preoccupation with sex has occurred not merely because the so-called Puritan or Victorian taboos of the past have been discarded. Rather, there now exists the patent toleration of every form of "sex tease" in a society incapable of developing uniform norms and patterns of conduct socially to channel the expression of this drive. The resulting combination of stimulation and confusion makes the problem presently acute. Loss or rejection of a common set of values paralyzes action in a democratic society, for there exist no widely accepted premises that can be applied in establishing practical programs of action.

The family experiences the effects of this situation in many ways. Parents recognize the greater need to instruct and guide their children in sexual matters, yet the majority feel hopelessly inadequate for the task. On their part, the schools in a pluralistic society must be content to disseminate only factual knowledge rather than codes of conduct. Meanwhile, modern youth is subjected to excessive tension, frustration, and uncertainty in their heterosexual relationships. They reach biological maturity many years before the accepted age for marriage, yet they are encouraged to engage in intimate and unsupervised dating and courtship practices at relatively early ages.

Family stability itself is adversely affected by the current tendency to emphasize only the physical aspects of sex. The conjugal act is an act of the person implying more than physical participation if it is to prove mutually unifying. The search for mere physical gratification results in sexual exploitation—a wholly different process from marital union in which the partners give themselves to each other in a culminating act of love. Yet a society that strongly emphasizes only the physical aspects of sex prepares many to seek little more than this personal gratification even in marriage. When spouses regard each other as sexual objects rather than as persons the mutual development and fulfillment which should be one of the major personal rewards of marriage is never achieved. This failure can have serious consequences in our modern, isolated domestic unit, which normally tends to place great emphasis on companionship and the development of mutual affection. In marriage, as in all other institutions, the primary source of disappointment and frustration is the non-achievement of expectations or aspirational goals.

Society's inability to develop an integrated view of the function of sex also gives rise to a series of discontinuities in the training and maturing process of American youth. The attitude toward sex stressed before marriage does not adequately prepare young people to take a mature view of sex in marriage. It may seem trite to point out that the reproductive drive in men and women is related to reproduction, and that, as a matter of fact, the majority of people who marry apparently desire to have children. Nevertheless, the prevalent segmented view of sex dissociates this normal purpose of the drive from its other aspects, so that there is little training and preparation for the roles of parenthood. Stated briefly, in the training of young people in our society great emphasis is placed on marriage, little on the family.

Closely related to the confusion concerning the function of sex is the variety of attitudes manifested toward the planning of family size. There are many reasons why the problem has become a critical issue. American couples tend to marry young and to start their families at once, thus increasing the span of years during which the wife is "exposed" to pregnancy. Because infant and child mortality rates are extremely low most children born will survive to maturity. Modern children are not only economically non-productive, they are definitely costly. Low infant mortality rates have been achieved by relatively expensive medical care and hospitalization. A technologically advanced society requires that children be supported during long years of formal education and training. When children are young their mother cannot increase the size of the family budget by following the modern pattern of seeking employment outside the home.

Moreover, because of mobility and changes in the family system, many young couples can no longer depend upon much help from their relatives during the childbearing and child-rearing stages of the family cycle. Hence, children in the family create special problems for parents in regard to renting, satisfactory room and play space, and proper neighborhood environment. Finally, the postwar baby boom, together with increased knowledge and interest in the population growth of the economically underdeveloped nations of Central and South America, Africa, and the Orient, has generated an outburst of propaganda advocating drastic and immediate control of population growth.

The solution most commonly advanced is some form of contraceptive birth control. As we have indicated, Catholics and some other religious groups consider the use of contraceptives morally objectionable. At the opposite pole are those who deny all moral content to the exercise of sex, so that the use of contraceptives is held to be an amoral, individual affair. Between these extremes appear various shades of thought distinguished primarily by the type of justification they postulate for legitimizing the practice. Despite these speculative differences it appears that some form of contraceptive birth control is widely practiced at one time or another by a large percentage of American families.

The practice serves a key function in co-ordinating biological necessities with socially acquired aspirations. Young couples plan their marriages in terms of birth control, while various elements in the social system such as early age at marriage, mothers in the work force, housing, family spending, and so forth, presuppose it.

In addition to the moral and wider social issues involved, the practice of birth control raises several questions related to marital success and happiness. In terms of the entire family cycle how well prepared are young couples to decide on the appropriate number of children they should have? It is frequently forgotten that the decision not to have another child has as much significance for the long range happiness of the couple as the decision to have one. Right reason in reproduction obviously implies control and choice, but the availability of relatively easy methods of control increases the responsibility of making an intelligent choice. There is little evidence in the prevalent piecemeal thinking on sex and marriage to indicate an awareness of this obligation even in terms of secular values. What psychological effects result from this practice? Does the conjugal act attempted under these conditions unify the couple and solidify the marriage bond? May we simply assume that an act of mutual gratification has the same significance and effects as the total gift of self in normal marital relations?

Most Americans are trained to believe that marriage should be monogamous and for life. Indeed, in some states the marriage license bears the text: "What God hath joined together, let no man put asunder." Yet our legal system renders little juridical support to family stability. Couples can enter a marriage contract and break it pretty much as they please. It is an open secret that in most states divorce can be obtained by mutual consent, for the average uncontested divorce is granted as a matter of course. This state of affairs is bound to create confusion. Young people are taught in their homes and at church that marriage is for life, yet through an open travesty of judicial procedure they see the contract easily dissolved, while the participants in the collusion apparently suffer no loss of social prestige.

We have already indicated that divorce becomes socially significant only when it is institutionalized. When this occurs other social relationships are geared to it; that is, marriages are contracted carelessly, marital adjustment loses some of its motivation, mutual fidelity is rendered more difficult, and an increasing number of spouses come to find their union intolerable. Even people who believe the marriage bond is indissoluble may be influenced by prevailing attitudes to the extent that they place personal goals above those of the family and do not hesitate to separate from their spouses if their aspirations are not adequately satisfied. For example, in one of our large dioceses, over two thousand Catholic couples separate each year.

It is worth pointing out that the prevalent confusion in modern attitudes toward divorce is symptomatic of a much more radical confusion concerning the nature of man. Because the human person is not viewed as basically social by nature, a false opposition has been assumed to exist between the individual and his social institutions. Hence, self-realization and the full development of personality are considered apart from society. Institutional restraints such as the marriage bond are regarded as limitations of individual freedom, to be endured only as the individual sees fit. This is the approach advanced by Rousseau, who posited man as a self-sufficient atom rather than as social by nature; consequently he regarded every institutional requirement as a restriction of man's freedom rather than as the necessary social framework for his development and fullest self-realization.

This assumption of Rousseau's runs through most arguments favoring divorce and greater individual freedom. We read a great deal about the need to allow for growth and development of personality, but we are given no definition of the person, so that the discussion of growth and development has no meaning in the context. Likewise, we are told that this development must take place within a framework of human cooperation and mutual concern for the freedom of others. This is merely to beg the whole question since we still have to define what institutional framework is required to secure co-operation and to guarantee respect for the freedom of others. In reality individual and institution are not opposed but mutually supportive. Because man is social by nature, institutional regulations such as fidelity and indissolubility in marriage are not limitations of developmental freedom but represent the necessary channeling of human social activity along lines in conformity with the fullest self-realization of the human person.

A further area of confusion is related to the definition of life goals. Our society offers no meaningful standards by which to judge success in life. When is a man a success? When has he "arrived"? In theory the "sky is the limit," and one advance merely sets the stage for another in a feverish, competitive climb to a "top" that is never clearly defined. In such a system the only socially recognized symbols of success are material objects—the things that you own or the money that you can afford to spend on what Thorstein Veblen called conspicuous consumption, that is, on showing off. Hence if we ask, "What makes them work so hard?" the answer is our competitive, open class system offering only its material symbols as guarantees of success.

This normless striving is reflected in family relationships. Some couples are so preoccupied with trying to keep up with or to surpass their neighbors that they overlook the possibilities for happiness in their immediate family circle. Marriage thus becomes little more than the conventional base of operations in an enduring competitive struggle. Under these circumstances children may come to be regarded as competitive pawns to show up the neighbors or as burdens limiting freedom and restricting the number of material symbols the couple can acquire. Wives may join in the competitive struggle by subtly prodding their husbands to strive for more rapid advancement, even at the cost of health and the sacrifice of human values, or they may by-pass their family obligations and enter the work force. Husbands, in turn, may rationalize their neglect of wife and children as a necessary consequence of their absorption in a business vocation that requires all of their time and energy if they are to advance according to expectations.

In other words, this segmented, ill-defined struggle for success inevitably results in the devaluation of family life. It is beside the point to blame technology or "the machine" for this state of affairs. These are but useful means, the products of which modern man has mistakenly erected into ultimate life goals. If the family has suffered devaluation, it is because our concentration on an ever higher standard of living and on the accumulation of the material symbols of success has blinded us to the human values and manifold opportunities for personal development that only the family can supply.

Nevertheless, in a society dominated by the market place it becomes difficult to develop a hierarchy of goals capable of integrating traditional family values, the ultimate purpose of life, and socially induced personal aspirations. In America, industrialization, with its accompanying technological advances, has been so rapid, so obviously successful, so all-absorbing that modern man is just starting to question its purpose in terms of human values and personal development. He now discovers that it has captivated our educational system, created many of the demands that it is built to supply, and established its own system of values and goals for which men strenuously compete as for their final purpose in life. Confusion will be dissipated and people will rediscover the significance of family life when they learn, as seemingly every age must learn anew, that the pursuit of happiness becomes meaningless and self-destructive unless it takes place in a framework of values based on the integral nature of man.

Religious leaders commonly designate this prevailing system of post-Christian attitudes and practices by the term *secularism*. In essence the term connotes a this-worldly, short-range philosophy of life that denies the practical implications of man's transcendent purpose and the existence of a divinely established objective moral order to which human conduct must conform. As we have indicated, it results in confusion because it supplies no reliable rule for integrating and ordering the varied goals for which men can strive. It presents a subtle threat to Christians, for though it really involves an implicit denial of man's basic dependence on his Creator, in its present guise it does not appear to involve a total rejection of belief in God. Rather, as Oscar Wilde cynically remarked, "Man has made God in his own image and likeness." Whether recognized or not, secularism assumes man's right to formulate his own definition of his relationship to his Creator. In the practical order this means that God is relegated to the vague role of first cause and final consoler.

Hence, secularism leaves no room for the traditional belief that God rules His creation through the natures of things and consequently that the divine plan can be discovered by studying these natures in their normal operations. To be sure, the majority of modern Christians are not inclined openly to reject traditional Christian family standards and ideals. Under the influence of secularism, however, they tend to argue, when special difficulties arise, that the achievement of these standards is impossible in their case—God requires no man to perform the impossible! Granting that these standards are excellent as ideals, modern conditions frequently make it impossible to live in accordance with them. Briefly, modern man tends to be intolerant of any moral restraint he cannot easily follow. Although admitting the possibility of sin in the speculative order, he insists on limiting objective morality to his personal, subjective capacities. By blandly ignoring man's ultimate purpose in life and his relationship of essential dependence on God secularism creates a climate of opinion encouraging even practicing Christians to engage in this convenient rationalization.

CHAPTER VII

Minority Problems

At one time or another most Catholics come to realize that they are members of a religious minority. They are made to feel somewhat like the little Mexican schoolboy in California who defined a minority as "somebody everyone else thinks is different—and worse." Whether it be in relation to Catholic education, divorce, birth control, mixed marriage, separation of Church and state, or fish on Friday, eventually the practicing Catholic recognizes that he is regarded as "different" and, at times, as "worse."

The personal experience of this fact may somewhat shock those Catholics whose previous associations have primarily involved fellow Catholics in a predominantly Catholic community, but they may realistically temper their surprise if they reflect that neither the Catholic nor the Jewish minorities have ever been fully accepted in American society. This is a matter of historical record which only the most naive observer of either the past or present would attempt to deny. More pertinent for present purposes is the realization that religious tension is not a one-way street. Misunderstanding, suspicion, and latent antipathy run in both directions, so that group tensions tend to be self-generating and self-perpetuating. As a result they are not easily handled even by mature persons, particularly when the situation requires close co-operation and intimate contact. A case in point is mixed marriage.

Out-group marriages pose a perennial threat to the survival of any cultural or religious minority. By its very nature marriage establishes an intimate bond of union readily transcending both minority cultural values and religious beliefs. Furthermore, since the marriage union is procreative, mixed marriages endanger the normal growth and continuity of a minority by limiting the acquisition of new members. Hence, minorities that possess a determination to survive have always used various means to prevent the dissipation of their forces and the dissolution of their traditions through out-group marriage.

Traditional Catholic opposition to mixed marriages is based on even more solid grounds. Experience shows that such unions endanger the faith of the Catholic partner as well as the religious training of children. No Catholic may lightly run the risk of losing his faith, nor may he enter marriage without assuming the serious obligation of raising his children in that faith. The Catholic position on mixed marriage is clearly stated in the Code of Canon Law and in various encyclicals. Centuries of experience, together with all modern research findings, leave no grounds for reasonable doubt concerning the dangers involved in such marriages.

There are several reasons why the problem of mixed marriages is regarded as peculiarly acute for modern American Catholics. The gap between Catholic family standards and those promoted in the dominant culture is rapidly increasing. On such moral issues as the use of contraceptives, the indissolubility of the marriage bond, and the sacramental nature of marriage Catholics maintain a doctrine clearly at variance with that held by the majority in American society. Further, the continued social and residential mobility of the Catholic population increases their opportunities for meeting those not of their faith. Contemporary dating and courtship practices make it possible for Catholics to become emotionally involved with non-Catholics even though valid marriage is out of the question or would prove extremely hazardous. Finally, although religious leaders have expressed strong opposition to such unions, both Catholics and non-Catholics alike appear amazingly indifferent to the dangers inherent in them.

A few preliminary definitions will help bring the problem in focus from the Catholic viewpoint. The Code distinguishes several types of marriage as follows: the union of two Catholics in a valid marriage; the union of a Catholic and a non-Catholic in a valid marriage. This is termed a mixed marriage and requires a dispensation from the bishop for the Catholic party. According to the Code there are two possible combinations: the union may involve a Catholic and a baptized non-Catholic (mixed religion) or a Catholic and an unbaptized non-Catholic (disparity of cult). Finally, there are invalid unions involving either two Catholic parties, a Catholic and a baptized non-Catholic, or a Catholic and a non-Christian.

Most important in discussing mixed marriages is the distinction between valid and invalid unions. Valid mixed marriages require a dispensation, which may be granted under the following conditions. There must be good and serious reasons, like avoiding a civil marriage, or a Protestant marriage, or concubinage, and so on. The non-Catholic party promises to remove all danger of perversion of the Catholic party, and both partners promise that all children born in the marriage shall be baptized and raised as Catholics. There is moral certainty that the promises will be kept. As a general rule the promises are to be made in writing. The Catholic party also has the obligation to work prudently for the conversion of the non-Catholic party. Even though a dispensation has been granted, the couple may not, either before or after the Catholic wedding, appear before a non-Catholic minister as such to give or renew their consent. Since valid marriages are celebrated with the permission of the Church fairly reliable records of such unions are preserved. Consequently, we can form a reasonable estimate of the number that take place during any given year.

Invalid mixed marriages are unions involving a Catholic and a non-Catholic for which no dispensation has been obtained. They are performed without the permission of the Church and are not recognized by the Church as marriages at all. The Catholic party is judged to be living in serious sin and is forbidden access to the sacraments as long as the union endures.

The Code places the added sanction of excommunication on the Catholic party if the marriage has been attempted before a non-Catholic minister as such. Excommunication is a censure by virtue of which a baptized person is excluded from the communion of the faithful and, among other effects, it deprives him of the use of the sacraments and Christian burial. Because invalid marriages are not performed in the Church they are not recorded by ecclesiastical authorities. At the same time, civil records do not indicate the religion of the parties to be married, with the result that the number of invalid marriages must be estimated from surveys and other indications.

What are the facts in regard to mixed marriages? Let us consider what we know about *valid* mixed marriages first. During the last two decades valid mixed marriages have accounted for approximately 30 per cent of all Catholic marriages. More Catholic women than men, in a ratio of about 60–40, enter valid mixed marriages. This suggests either that Catholic boys are more successful in converting their non-Catholic partners or that they more readily enter invalid unions. There are indications that the latter hypothesis is correct.

The rates of all types of mixed marriages increase during periods of war. Throughout the country there are wide regional differences in rates, and even within the same diocese, rates may differ considerably from parish to parish.

What external factors are associated with these varied rates? The most obvious one is the percentage of Catholics in the total population of the area. Valid mixed marriage rates run as high as 70 per cent where Catholics are few; they drop to below 10 per cent where Catholics are numerous. However, this is not the only factor related to difference in rates. The percentage of such marriages tends to be higher among Catholics in the higher socio-economic brackets. It is lowest among those national minorities who still remain clustered around their original parish settlements or who still retain strong national solidarity.

How stable are valid mixed marriages? Several studies conducted in widely separated areas of the country seem to prove
conclusively that they are much more unstable than marriages
involving partners of the same faith. Unfortunately the value of
these studies is seriously limited by the facts that they dealt
only with those mixed marriages in which there were children
of school age and that they did not distinguish between valid
and invalid unions. However, several intensive parish studies
indicate that mixed marriages are much less stable than marriages involving two Catholics, and general observation backs
up their findings.

Why are these marriages less stable? It is generally assumed
that they will break up because of quarrels over religion or over
the religious training of children. Undoubtedly such quarrels
occur frequently and account for some breakdowns, but in a
study of 1,284 broken mixed marriages we found that adultery
accounted for over 50 per cent of the failures and direct quarrels
over religion for only about 10 per cent.

Our findings point up an important consequence of religious
differences in marriage. Most couples find it impossible to discuss such differences calmly. They may start out by trying to
be very mature and even sophisticated about it all, but before
long one or both of them realize it is not so easy to be matter-
of-fact when discussing differences in religious beliefs. Emo-
tions enter in very quickly. Church loyalty, childhood preju-
dices, misinformation—all gang up to make any discussion of
religion far from a comfortable undertaking even among lovers.
After a few attempts most couples silently agree to disagree.
But the differences continue to keep them apart. In practice
these will appear as essential disagreements over the nature
and purposes of marriage itself. Quarrels will consequently
center on family limitation, marital infidelity, and so forth,
rather than on religion as such.

Do mixed marriages affect the religious practice of the Catholic partner? All reliable research findings on this problem are
conclusive, so there can be little doubt about the harmful effects

of such unions. To summarize our own findings, covering thousands of cases drawn from different sections of the country, roughly 25 per cent of the Catholics involved in valid mixed marriages had severed all connection with the Church, another 20 per cent attended church services only sporadically, and only the remaining 55 per cent could be classified as practicing Catholics.

What happens to the religious training of the children in such marriages? Here again the findings are conclusive. Although children tend to fare somewhat better in mixed marriages involving a Catholic mother, the over-all picture is appalling. Speaking conservatively, we conclude on the basis of our extensive research that roughly 40 per cent of all children born to such marriages are either unbaptized, or are baptized as Protestants, or are baptized as Catholics but receive no formal instruction in the faith.

It is difficult to obtain adequate information concerning invalid mixed marriages. Not only are such cases not recorded by the Church, but our information on invalid marriages does not always tell us the grounds for the invalidity. We have pointed out that Catholic marriages may be invalid for a variety of reasons, so that some of the invalid marriages studied will probably not be mixed marriages. This fact should be kept in mind when considering some of the following data. There is ample evidence to show that a surprising percentage of Catholics are involved in invalid marriages. For example, an analysis of the dispensations granted for mixed marriages reveals that between 20 and 30 per cent of these marriages had originally been contracted invalidly. Further, a study of all the mixed marriages in 132 parishes located in the East and Middle West showed that approximately 40 per cent of these marriages were invalid. Finally, each of the major diocesan chancery courts handles several hundred "defect of form" cases each year. It will be recalled that these are cases in which a Catholic has been involved in an invalid marriage, has secured a civil divorce, and now wishes to contract a valid marriage in the Church. Since a good percentage of invalid marriages apparently do not end in divorce, the fact that chancery courts handle such large numbers of "defect of form" cases indicates that the total number of invalid marriages must be surprisingly high.

What are the effects of such invalid unions? We have already indicated that the Catholic parties are judged to be living in sin, and if the ceremony has taken place in the presence of a non-Catholic minister they are excommunicated. This means they are entirely cut off from the life of the Church. How stable are such unions? Obviously there is great moral pressure on the Catholic party either to get the marriage validated or to break up the union. As we have shown, many of these unions are validated each year. There is good evidence to suggest that a considerable number eventually break up. In a study of 6,744 divorces involving Catholics we found that approximately 60 per cent were invalid unions. This indicates that such unions are relatively unstable, for invalid marriages are only a relatively small proportion of all marriages involving Catholics, yet they accounted for 60 per cent of all divorces.

What do we know about the baptism and religious training of children in these unions? The Catholic parent has a grave and enduring obligation to raise the children in the Catholic faith and he incurs excommunication if he agrees to have them baptized or brought up in a non-Catholic sect. But as one student of the problem stated on the basis of his lifelong experience, it was possible to predict with mathematical accuracy that 60 per cent of the children of such unions would never be baptized and that only a small percentage would ever attend a Catholic school. Our surveys verify this dire prediction. These results are not surprising, however, since Catholics involved in such unions either have no strong religious convictions, or are completely under the domination of the non-Catholic partner, or find themselves incapable of facing the trying experience of having their children baptized and entered in a Catholic school.

What predictions can be made about future trends in mixed marriage? Although all prediction is hazardous, there are many reasons to conclude that the rates for both valid and invalid mixed marriages will increase. We have already pointed out the widespread indifference to the dangers inherent in mixed marriages among Catholics and non-Catholics alike. We have noted the increasing vertical and horizontal mobility of the American Catholic population. The resultant increased contact with non-Catholics, further facilitated by modern means of communication and our contemporary dating and courtship practices, greatly increases the likelihood of mixed marriages. At the same time, the solidarity of our large national minorities, which has hitherto operated as a strong check on out-group marriage, is gradually undergoing disintegration as members of these groups move away from their original settlement around the national parish.

Furthermore, there is some evidence that mixed marriages have a cumulative effect. The children of these unions tend to marry outside their religious group more often than do the offspring of in-group marriages. This would seem to be a result of increased contacts with non-Catholics and permissive parental attitudes both toward such contacts and toward mixed marriage itself.

Likewise, the continued high rate of divorce in America offers a growing threat to members of the Catholic minority in terms of invalid marriage. The present divorce rate is turning between 700,000 and 800,000 divorced persons loose in American society each year. Apparently the great majority of these divorced persons eventually remarry. In the light of the factors we have enumerated above, there seems every possibility that an increasing number of Catholics may become involved in such remarriages. Since the majority of first marriages appear to be valid, marriage with either a divorced Catholic or a divorced non-Catholic will be invalid.

How are Catholics to meet this challenge to their family system? Granting that the individual Catholic alone is responsible for the decision to enter such a union, in terms of long-range policy future trends will depend primarily on how Catholic parents fulfill their obligations. They alone have some control over the dating and courtship patterns of their children, and in the final analysis it is they who mold their children's basic attitudes toward religious values. Hence, Catholic parents must recognize and clearly understand the serious hazards that mixed marriages necessarily involve. Only if they are thoroughly convinced themselves can they train their children in the conviction that differences in religious beliefs create fundamental differences in value systems which love cannot resolve. Briefly, here are some of the ideas that they will stress in forming the attitudes of their children toward mixed marriages.

On such moral issues as the use of contraceptive birth control, the indissolubility of the marriage bond, the seriousness of infidelity, and the sacramental nature of marriage Catholics maintain a doctrine quite distinct from many others in our society. These issues are rationally solved on the basis of belief, not love.

The religious training of children can be the source of conflict even when a couple are very much in love. The Church insists that the children be trained as Catholics and that where there are Catholic schools, the children attend them. It would surprise no one that the non-Catholic partner may find this obligation difficult to accept once children have arrived.

Even though the influence of relatives is diminishing in our modern family system, immediate relatives still exert a good deal of pressure on the individual when religious differences are involved. In-law interference may appear positively by attempting to control the religious affiliation and training of children, and negatively by excluding the divergent partner from full acceptance in the family group.

Church loyalties frequently become the source of quarrels. All organized religious groups demand time, interest, and money of their members. When husband and wife have different church loyalties, the door is open to disagreements that are not easily resolved because they are founded on emotion-loaded religious beliefs and habits.

Above all, mixed marriages seriously compromise the intimate, spiritual unity of marriage. According to the Catholic ideal, marriage is a life partnership and companionship in which each partner supports and works for the temporal and spiritual welfare of the other. In mixed marriages religion is more likely to be a bone of contention than a unifying bond. The Catholic spouse must pray alone, attend church services alone, go up to the Communion rail alone; in short, he retains a whole world of spiritual experiences and values that he cannot share with the one person in the world who should be closest to him.

Catholic parents must realize that most young people are too inexperienced to evaluate adequately the hazards of mixed marriage. They require instruction and patient guidance. Inasmuch as dating frequently leads to courtship and courtship to marriage, parents must make every effort to see that their children associate with Catholic friends. It is a little late to start discussing the dangers of mixed marriage after young people have fallen in love. Perhaps most important in the long run, parents must carefully foster in their children a deep appreciation of the dignity and beauty of Christian marriage as a life vocation in the service of God. Of course Church and school can assist parents in developing all of the points above, but experience shows that they are singularly incapable of effecting much unless parents fulfill their obligations adequately.

In the last chapter we pointed out that sex constitutes one of the major modern areas of confusion and disagreement. This stems from the implicit or explicit rejection of the traditional Christian viewpoint. Confusion is revealed at the level of conduct in the relatively unrestricted exploitation of sex in advertising, recreation, entertainment, and so forth; in the toleration, if not promotion, of sexual license especially before marriage; and in the widespread acceptance and use of contraceptive birth control practices. Implicit in this conduct is the assumption of two new postulates concerning human sexual activity. The first divorces the function of sex from its primary reproductive purpose, while the second takes sexual activity out of the realm of morality so that its proper expression need no longer be judged in terms of an objective moral order. Further analysis of this new conception of sex reveals that it really involves an implicit denial of man's basic dependence on his Creator.

According to the Catholic viewpoint the order of right reason must be realized in sex as in all areas of human activity. Briefly, what does the order of reason require? It demands that the primary purpose of sex should be respected in its use. It insists that the inner structure of the moral person should be kept intact. This means that the spiritual has primacy over the physical in the aspirations and activities of man. It maintains that justice between men be observed. This underlines the social significance of sex, for man possesses sex not primarily for his personal use, but as a privilege enabling him to share in the creative activity of God.

This Christian concept of sex is so comprehensive, balanced, and consistent with human experience that Catholics should have little difficulty in developing sane attitudes and practices. Unfortunately this is not always the case. In regard to sex some Christians almost imply that the Creator, like the poet Homer, must have nodded at times. As a result, certain tendencies in Catholic thinking about sex have created a situation in which many are poorly prepared to meet the current challenge.

Much of the difficulty many Catholics encounter in treating sex rationally stems from a subtle error, the misplacement or misdirection of moral anger. This error is so basic that we shall treat its speculative and practical consequences at some length. By the misdirection of moral anger we mean simply that the

Christian's natural disgust and hatred for an offense against God has been misdirected. This error results from a confusion of sins against chastity and the physical manifestations of sex. The quality of sinfulness has been mistakenly extended from the prohibited act to the physical phenomena. Because the conscious, deliberate consent to venereal pleasure under morally forbidden circumstances constitutes sin, some people have erroneously attributed the quality of sinfulness to the venereal pleasure itself and to the physical organs that give rise to it. Hence, there has developed a tendency to regard the physical aspects of sex as sinful and to lose sight of the fact that the sinfulness of unchaste actions is a quality of the act of consent, not of the venereal pleasure involved. This extension of sinfulness to the physical aspects of sex has serious speculative consequences.

It perverts the Catholic doctrine of sin, leaving the door wide open to the age-old heresy of Manichaeism, which sees something inherently evil in matter itself. Catholic doctrine maintains that sin consists in the conscious, deliberate choice to act contrary to God's will as the individual knows it. The physical world is not evil, though it may be used for evil purposes. Considered in themselves, sexual stimulation and pleasure are morally indifferent; it is the decision to use them contrary to right order that constitutes sin. By attributing sinfulness to the physical aspects of sex, one perverts Catholic doctrine regarding the nature of sin and promotes the essentially un-Christian attitude that bodily or physical phenomena are evil.

This error leads to a distorted view of chastity. Because the physical elements of sex are considered evil there is a tendency to consider the chaste person as some type of sexless creature, a person who never experiences the physical expression of sex rather than one who always uses his sexual powers in accord with God's plan. Mere physical integrity comes to be considered a value in itself; the implicit assumption is made that chastity applies primarily to the unmarried.

This error leads to a non-Christian view of the human person. It is based on a false separation between the physical or corporal and the spiritual elements in man. Sexual acts are considered "carnal," "animal," or expressions of man's "lower nature." Catholic doctrine maintains that man is a unity composed of two co-principles, the material and the spiritual. Conscious human acts cannot be merely "carnal," or "animal," or of man's "lower nature." It is the human person who acts in all cases. Thus, it is not our body that feels, it is we who feel. It is not our mind that thinks, it is we who think. In our conscious activities we always act as a human person, that is, as a composite being, a body-soul unity. Those who speak disparagingly of sex, therefore, imply an unreal divorce between the two co-principles in human nature. Their attitude is especially harmful because they deprive sex of its meaning and dignity.

Well-intentioned Christians, no doubt, have initiated this "smear campaign" against sex in the hope that they could dissuade people from sinning against chastity and in order to strengthen personal self-control. Paradoxically, experience shows that they have accomplished neither of these purposes, for their approach deprives the sexual drive of none of its force, while it does destroy its human significance. We do not eliminate reality by denying its existence or by giving it a dirty name. The Christian approach is to bring sex under the control of right reason, thus enabling it to fulfill its purpose for human perfection.

This error has also resulted in an unbalanced stress on what might be termed the negative aspects of the virtue of chastity. Major emphasis is placed on what not to do. Chastity comes to be regarded as a series of "don'ts." The relationships between chastity and modesty are not clearly explained, with the result that some actions are arbitrarily judged sinful rather than as possible occasions of sin. Because the nature and function of sex seldom receives a positive, integrated treatment, everything connected with sex becomes rather vague, indefinite, a source of worry and anxiety, if not of actual disgust. Yet the positive assertion of the sexual impulse in the individual's life remains, so that people must develop a whole series of rationalizations, subterfuges, and disguises for dealing with it. The subject of sex comes to be regarded as a kind of secret, to be discussed in whispers or behind closed doors but never to be brought out in the open and appraised in accord with right reason and Catholic doctrine.

Finally, this error has led to a partial, segmented view of the nature of sex. When thinking centers on the physical aspects of the sex drive there is a tendency to ignore or pass over in silence the inherent qualities of manliness and womanliness that the possession of sex implies. We read in the Bible that God created man "male and female" as companions and helpmates. Each possesses characteristic complementary qualities which must be actualized if their personalities are to be fully developed in marriage. These qualities are related to their different reproductive roles, but they extend far beyond them. Sex endows men and women with distinctive physical, emotional, psychic, and spiritual qualities enabling them to complete each other as companions and co-partners in the family enterprise of childbearing and child rearing. Hence, overemphasis, disparaging or otherwise, on the merely physical aspects of sex destroys its integral meaning. Its extensive complementary qualities are undervalued or ignored, with the result that in modern marriage there is frequently competition rather than co-operation, cohabitation without companionship.

What are the practical consequences of this error? They generally appear as negative attitudes to the facts of life. Let us consider a few of them. Because parents regard everything related to sex as somehow "dirty," "nasty," and peculiarly "unladylike," they find it difficult to give their children the instruction necessary to aid them in developing the integral virtue of chastity. Under these circumstances young people are driven to questionable sources in the normal quest for knowledge. Parental attitudes foster the impression that sex is something that cannot be dealt with intelligently; the virtue of chastity is reduced to a meaningless negation; the physical aspects of sex are not related to the sublime privilege of parenthood; and the puzzling, persistent, gradually developing assertion of sexual power appears as a source of worry and anxiety. Growing youth is confused by its novelty and power, yet perplexed by the need for its rational control.

This negative approach is clearly revealed in parental attitudes toward dating and courtship. Failure to face openly and intelligently the phenomena of sex and its significance causes many parents to act as if their growing children were sexless creatures or at least quite above "such things." Hence, they tolerate and even promote premarital relationship patterns that are normally calculated to induce considerable sexual arousal. Although young people in our society become biologically mature many years before marriage is a social possibility, they are frequently urged to start the dating process at an early age. As a result their problems are multiplied and many tend to rush into marriage before they are ready to assume its responsibilities.

This negative approach to sex likewise hinders intelligent preparation for marriage. Since the primary purpose of marriage is the procreation and education of children, it would appear logical to conclude that adequate training for marriage would involve some preparation for the fulfillment of this function. Because parents do not teach their girls to view their womanliness in terms of motherhood and boys their manliness in terms of fatherhood, young couples enter marriage with slight consideration for the implications of parenthood. It is not surprising that some young wives regard pregnancy as an inevitable misfortune rather than a normal fulfillment of womanhood. Children are regarded as burdens rather than blessings. Their care becomes unnecessarily onerous when parents are prepared neither in attitudes nor practical techniques for their responsibilities.

Finally, this negative approach hinders adjustment in marriage. Men and women enter marriage without an adequate appreciation of its primary purpose. Because they have not been trained to take a positive, rational view of sex they find it difficult to understand the Church's teaching that the use of contraceptives is contrary to the divine plan. Mutual understanding is hindered, since the spouses find it difficult to express or discuss their intimate feelings, needs, or desires. A couple's negative attitudes are not miraculously made positive by the wedding ceremony. Marital relations do not increase mutual love and promote the enrichment of personality when they are regarded merely as an obligation by one and a self-centered right by the other.

We have discussed this error in some detail because it deeply and subtly permeates much current thinking. The misdirection of moral anger is based on a heresy that has plagued the mind of man down through history. It crops up most often in regard to sex, for this basic drive is not easily brought under the control of reason. Yet it is precisely because sexual power is so noble and necessary, enabling man to co-operate with God in His creative activity, that it requires the preserving and protecting order of reason. As St. Thomas reminds us: "The more necessary something is, the more the order of reason must be preserved in it." Hence, if Catholics are to meet the current sex "revolution," their first step is to recheck their attitudes in order to make certain that they are thinking "with the Church." This balanced, integrated, positive view offers them the principles that must be applied in working out practical programs of action under conditions of rapid change.

Catholics must also acquire a greater awareness of what we have called the social implications of their ideals. They cannot hope to actualize the divine plan for sex in their lives if they thoughtlessly follow prevalent attitudes and practices related to modesty and chastity. Above all, they must be profoundly convinced of the need for divine assistance. The faithful following of Christ is impossible without constant recourse to prayer and the sacraments. No sane Christian would deny this, yet it is easily forgotten in a society that relegates religion to Sunday church services and a few major events such as baptisms, weddings, and funerals.

In the last chapter we indicated some of the social factors that have caused the problem of planning family size to become acute. Although the solution adopted by American society is morally objectionable to Catholic couples there is sufficient evidence to indicate that some are deviating from Christian ideals in this area, while others manifest tension and strain. Before offering suggestions designed to meet this issue in terms of Catholic principles, let us review briefly how the problem presents itself to Catholic couples.

As members of American society they will tend to marry young and to start their families early in marriage. Those who are mobile will be seriously preoccupied with accumulating the material symbols of success as defined in better housing and living standards for themselves and more ample educational opportunities for their children. Even those who are not anxiously striving to advance their social status discover that "keeping up with the Joneses" in their neighborhood requires constant effort.

These are legitimate aspirations, but since Catholic couples may not arbitrarily limit the size of their families, some may feel considerably handicapped in this competitive struggle. If God blesses them with numerous children they are bound to experience strain in trying to maintain their social position and to provide for their growing family in a modern urban environment. Under these circumstances the problem they face is not so much the rejection of contraceptive practices on moral grounds as the acceptance of the consequences of this rejection in a society that is geared to these practices. Caught in a contradictory series of social needs and moral demands, they are likely to feel frustrated and penalized because of their religious beliefs.

How can Catholic couples meet this situation? Obviously the solution must be worked out in terms of Christian principles, but there are several reasons why this may not prove an easy task for American Catholics. The negative attitudes toward sex that many have developed hinder them from integrating sexual expression with their service of God and their own personal fulfillment. Even in marriage, sex may be regarded as a thing apart, a necessity of nature, a mutually rewarding personal experience perhaps, but not a mutually perfecting activity designed for the service of God. Consequently, when conformity to Catholic moral standards requires serious sacrifice, these standards may be rejected or considered not pertinent under modern conditions. Because previous training has led them to regard the whole area of sex as something vague, negative, more or less irrational, and under considerable suspicion they find it relatively easy to by-pass the application of right reason to it in marriage.

At the same time, as Catholic couples begin to experience the full impact of an increasingly alien culture, they are forced to make choices among competing family norms and practices for which their previous training may have given them little preparation. Why are they poorly prepared? Many Catholics tend to show little interest in ultimate principles and the logical relationships between these and approved conduct. They remain fully satisfied with practical conclusions and applications, with the result that they are unable to offer "reasons for the faith that is in them." This non-intellectual approach leaves them unprepared either to meet change in terms of Christian principles or to withstand the subtle, morally dissipating influence of daily contact with widely accepted alien practices.

How can we remedy this intellectual apathy? The first step must be a serious revaluation of traditional methods of religious indoctrination. Whether through historical accident or unreflecting intent, much of Catholic religious education, preaching, and writing has emphasized specific norms and patterns of conduct without consistently relating these to the ultimate principles upon which they are necessarily based. Too many Catholics seem to regard obligatory practices in terms of arbitrary authority rather than in terms of absolute principles and their logical applications to the practical order. Catholic family standards are thus viewed as a collection of disparate rules and regulations (no divorce, no birth control, and so on) and not as an integrated system. But deprived of their value referents, many Catholic family standards appear meaningless or as the mere impositions of religious authority rather than the practical implementation of an accepted Christian philosophy of life.

It follows that programs that stress practices while neglecting to emphasize ultimate principles will be ineffective in the long run. Catholic family standards have meaning primarily in terms of the integral Christian philosophy of life. There is little likelihood that Catholic couples will continue to observe the former unless they are deeply imbued with the latter, for they live in a pluralistic society which lends their family values little support and sharply challenges them at many points.

Hence, inasmuch as every rational program of action represents a conclusion based on the application of premises of values to a set of social facts we must formulate a thoughtful restatement of the meaning and significance of the marriage vocation in terms of Catholic values *and* contemporary living conditions. In other words, Catholic couples must be trained to recognize and appreciate the necessary relationship between the Christian values they profess to believe and their practical conduct in marriage. They need to understand that legitimate aspirations for success and happiness in marriage can be fully realized only within the framework of the Creator's plan. As rational beings they must recognize that all their attitudes, values, and goals can be rightly ordered only in terms of their ultimate purpose in life. Finally, their faith must be deepened and, in the words of St. Paul, "stirred up" so that they enjoy the profound conviction that the sacramental graces available to them offer sufficient strength for carrying out their marital obligations even under conditions calling for considerable daily sacrifice.

Such reappraisal is necessary not only because contemporary society lacks a Christian outlook. Equally important is the fact that traditional viewpoints and definitions were formulated to meet different social conditions and may lack realism and cogency for the modern couple. Current research reveals that some young couples raised in a conservative Catholic environment appear ill-prepared to meet the challenge to Catholic family standards. Because their religious practice appears to have been based on mere custom rather than on intelligent conviction they seem incapable of interpreting new situations in terms of the religious values they still profess. As a result they tend to retain only those religious practices that cost them relatively little, while they overlook the radical contradiction in their conduct because they have not been trained to understand the necessary relationship between behavior and belief.

In this connection it is well to note that many couples fail to recognize the real implications of many modern changes related to sex and marriage. They apparently regard all changes, whether in the area of economics, politics, social customs, fashions, or morals, as more or less inevitable. If adjustment to modern change requires the rejection of some traditional Catholic standards, then these must go—for God does not ask the impossible! Such couples frequently soothe their consciences by arguing that moral theologians are typically slow in meeting contemporary problems. Traditional solutions may have worked very well in a simple, rural society; today they are no longer pertinent. Eventually the "Church" will catch up with the modern world; meanwhile, modern couples decide they will just have to work out their family problems in their own way.

It should be noted that a true appreciation of the Christian family ideal logically implies an appreciation of the means necessarily required to implement this ideal in the practical order. If one desires a goal or end, one must logically desire the means required to achieve it. This implies that Catholics as individuals and as a group, in co-operation with all other like-minded citizens, must do all that lies in their power to counteract the conditions that render family life unduly burdensome for some couples in modern society. This involves adequate provision for housing, health care, wages, and so forth. It involves realistic preparation of young men and women for marriage and parenthood. It involves the restoration of social charity—the rekindling of that primitive Christian spirit of mutual responsibility which once caused the contemporary pagans to exclaim, "See how these Christians love one another!" This spirit must be reactivated in the family circle, among relatives, neighbors, and members of the parish, so that the reality of brotherhood in Christ, of the Mystical Body, once again becomes visibly operative.

We pointed out that the real break with traditional Christian family standards came about with the denial of the sacramental nature of the marriage bond. The current consequences of this denial are revealed in the social acceptance and prevalence of divorce, together with the growing rate of invalid marriages. In a sense the relatively high rate of valid mixed marriages indicates a lack of appreciation of the sacrament inasmuch as the Catholic party chooses to enter a life partnership with one who does not recognize and consequently cannot appreciate its sacramental nature.

What does this denial of the sacramental nature of marriage imply? Obviously for Catholics it indicates either rejection, ignorance, or little appreciation of the supernatural life as defined by the teaching Church. In the final analysis it reveals either a speculative or practical rejection of the Christian philosophy of life and the Church's divine mission in the world. Lest we appear to be exaggerating the profound significance of this denial let us enlarge upon this observation briefly.

The human situation as the Church defines it is that man is separated from God by sin. Because of the Fall, unredeemed man remains alienated from his Creator, powerless to achieve his final purpose in life which is union with God. To solve this human dilemma, the Church offers Christ—as teacher, as victim for sin, and as mediator between God and man. Now Catholics who reject or ignore the sacramental nature of marriage and consequently the significance of supernatural life display a profound misconception of the human situation as revealed by faith. Their action indicates that they have no real understanding of human nature—man as a composite of body and soul, man as a sharer in the natural and supernatural, man historically separated from God by sin, man standing in need of redemption and regeneration. It follows that they can have no true appreciation of the mission of Christ and His Church since only within the framework of this conception of human nature can the significance of these be understood.

We have stressed the implications of this denial of the sacramental nature of marriage because they are frequently overlooked in formulating family programs. People tend to regard deviations from Catholic moral standards as mere indications of human weakness and recalcitrance. No doubt some of them are, and they must be handled accordingly. However, when deviations become widespread we are forced to assume that other factors are operative. We suggest that a rejection or misconception of the Catholic view of life is really involved.

How can this situation be remedied? In reviewing past teaching and preaching practices related to marriage, one might well question whether the subtle, pervasive, religiously alien influences shaping the thinking of the Catholic minority in our society have not been all too frequently ignored. In other words, it can no longer be assumed that because couples profess to be Catholics they have an adequate understanding and appreciation of Catholic family standards and life goals. From childhood on, American Catholics are subjected to a variety of confusing and contradictory cultural forces which tend to dull their keen perception of spiritual values. Consequently arguments stressing grace and the supernatural often fall on spiritually dull ears. Such arguments imply integrated, long-range thinking, while their audience is living under the tyranny of the segmented present.

In short, there is little to be gained by repeating the Church's solution to family problems if the supporting framework of doctrine is no longer meaningful. Catholics need a vivid awareness of the essential human dilemma—man separated from God by sin. They need a frequent reminder of the four last things: heaven, hell, death, and the judgment. This is not a plea for a return to a sterile hell-fire approach, but a reminder that the neglect or soft-pedaling of basic dogma inevitably results in the loss of deep religious conviction. Religious belief and practice are bound to become superficial and mere matters of custom if there is no clear understanding of the essential problems of human existence which only religion can answer.

It has always been one of the chief teaching functions of the Church to remind men in every age of their fallen nature, of their need for redemption, of their essential purpose in life; and in terms of these to offer Christ as the solution. This function requires special stress today because the chaos and disorder of the modern world, together with blind faith in the natural and social sciences, have created a climate of opinion that defines the human situation as basically one of conflict with nature or with society. It is assumed that the essential human dilemma can be solved by subduing nature and by developing the science of human relations. Progress will come, we are told, from the energetic exploitation of nature's resources and from the intelligent application of the techniques of adjustment and adaptation to modern life now being developed.

This profound misconception of the human situation has fairly captivated the modern mind. Despite the splendid achievements in the sciences that it inspires, however, it offers no basis for the solution of the human dilemma because it does not understand the nature of the problem. More serious, it has oriented the energy and interests of men toward the pursuit of partial and ephemeral goals, with the result that men's preoccupation with the achievement of these has kept them from investigating the real dimensions of the human problem. Under these conditions, religion is regarded as no more than a convenient social vehicle for promoting good human relations and group solidarity. It provides no ultimate answers because men turn to it for the solution of no basic problems.

CHAPTER VIII

Family Programs

There is some danger that our description of the confusion concerning sex and marriage in American society, together with our outline of the special family problems facing Catholic couples, will leave the impression that the American family system is about to disintegrate. This was hardly our intent, though the demands of our task required considerable emphasis on the least satisfactory aspects of the over-all picture. In reality there exists a balanced, stable core of healthy families among all the major religious groups as well as among the unchurched. If this were not the case such groups would soon cease to exist, while the American social system would face inevitable collapse.

By channeling the sexual drive, by providing for the procreation and education of children, and by serving as the prime social vehicle for the adequate transmission of the cultural heritage the family fulfills a set of highly essential functions, so that no religious or social group can long endure unless a good percentage of the family units that comprise them remain fundamentally vital and successful. Confusion and instability related to family life are consequently always a matter of degree. Although a family system is not necessarily self-correcting, like any other essential social institution it either achieves a basic minimum of success, or the group faces anarchy and disintegration. It follows that an analysis of unhealthy family trends, potential factors of instability, and basic sources of disagreement is highly relevant for all American citizens. Such analysis assumes particular pertinence for members of a religious minority who seek to preserve a distinctive set of family ideals and standards.

Fortunately, there is a brighter side to the picture. Granted that some current conditions present serious challenges, it is stimulating to record the vigorous response of many contemporary couples. They are not merely interested in preserving their marriages; they desire to make them outstanding successes. As husbands and wives they no longer take themselves for granted; as parents they earnestly seek better ways to fulfill their roles. Perhaps at no time in recent history have so many Catholic couples reacted so energetically to the perennial threat of mediocrity.

There can be little doubt that much of the renewed popular interest in the plight of the family has been occasioned by a growing awareness that not all is well on the family front. The high incidence of divorce, juvenile delinquency, and sexual immorality is becoming a matter of national concern. In this connection it is pertinent to note that the fate of the family under the impact of industrialism passed almost unnoticed during the nineteenth century. Auguste Comte, the founder of modern sociology, emphasized the importance of the family, but his followers tended to ignore this element of his teaching. Hence, with the exception of the French Catholic sociologist Pierre Le Play, social scientists paid little attention to the adverse effects of industrialization on the family system. Though we have made some advances today, the fundamental significance of the family for a stable social system is recognized in theory more than in practice. The extent of urban and rural slums in a country that boasts of its wealth and technological "know-how" shows that as a nation we still have little practical understanding of the importance of healthy family life.

Perhaps the two chief sources inspiring Catholic couples to take a renewed interest in family-life programs are the relatively recent papal statements emphasizing marriage as a means of mutual sanctification and the role of the laity in the apostolic work of the Church. In 1930 Pius XI published his classic encyclical *On Christian Marriage*. One passage in particular, his analysis of domestic love, supplies considerable understanding of the inspiration and enthusiasm displayed in contemporary Catholic family movements:

The love, then, of which we are speaking is not that based on the passing lust of the moment nor does it consist in pleasing words only, but in the deep attachment of the heart which is expressed in action, since love is proved by deeds. This outward expression of love in the home demands not only mutual help but must go further, indeed, must have its primary purpose that man and wife help each other day by day in forming and perfecting themselves in the interior life; so that through their partnership in life they may advance ever more in virtue, and above all that they may grow in true love towards God and their neighbor on which indeed "dependeth the whole law and the prophets." For all men, of every condition and in whatever honorable walk of life they may be, can and ought to imitate that most perfect example of holiness, placed before man by God, namely, Christ Our Lord, and by God's grace to arrive at the summit of perfection, as is proved by the example of many saints.

This mutual inward moulding of husband and wife, this determined effort to perfect each other, can in a very real sense, as the Roman Catechism teaches, be said to be the chief reason and purpose of matrimony, provided matrimony be looked at not in the restricted sense as instituted for the proper conception and education of the child, but more widely as the blending of life as a whole and the mutual interchange and sharing thereof.

By this same love it is necessary that all the other rights and duties of the marriage state be regulated so that the words of the Apostle, "Let the husband render the debt to the wife, and the wife also in like manner to the husband," express not only a law of justice but a norm of charity.

This emphasis on the integration of domestic love with the constant effort to strive for Christian perfection answered a profound modern need. Catholics have always believed that marriage is a vocation leading to perfection in the service of God, but perhaps under the impact of secularism, emphasis in teaching tended to focus on the refutation of current errors rather than on the positive aspects of married life. Meanwhile, the increase of the relatively isolated, small family type had intensified the modern couple's aspiration for "oneness" and heightened their sensitivity to intimate family relationships. By pointing out the essential connection between Christian domestic love and the search for perfection the Pope showed modern couples how they could convert their increased companionship into an effective process of mutual sanctification.

The second source of inspiration for Catholic couples has been the modern emphasis on the role of the laity in the Church. Recent popes, in particular Pius XI and Pius XII, have been tireless in urging the active participation of the laity in the apostolate of the hierarchy. This obligation stems from membership in the Mystical Body of Christ and from the divinely established structure of the Church, but its special urgency today is related to the minority position that Catholics maintain in a highly secularized society. Pius XII, speaking to a newly appointed group of cardinals in 1946, spoke of the Church's mission and the role of the laity in it as follows:

. . . Considered from this angle, the Church may be called the assembly of those who, under the supernatural influence of grace, in the perfection of their personal dignity as sons of God and in the harmonious development of all human inclinations and energies, build the powerful structure of human relationships.

Under this aspect, Venerable Brethren, the faithful, and

more precisely, the laity, are in the front line of the Church's life; for them the Church is the vital principle of human society. Accordingly they—especially they—must have an ever clearer sense not only of belonging to the Church, but of being the Church, the community of the Faithful on earth under the guidance of the common head, the Pope, and of the Bishops in communion with Him (*The Function of the Church*).

The call to lay action has not gone unheeded. Not only in formally organized Catholic Action groups but in a multitude of other ways, the laity have sprung into action. Most pertinent to our present purposes is the activity manifested on the family front. Numerous groups, focusing on a variety of specific goals and employing a diversity of means, have been either reactivated, reoriented, or newly formed. They range from the small, relatively simple units like the La Leche society, established by women in some cities to encourage breast-feeding and better infant care, to the large, complex, multi-purposed organizations like Cana and the Christian Family Movement. At the national level the Bishops have established the Family Life Bureau of the National Catholic Welfare Conference to unify, co-ordinate, and promote family-life activities throughout the country. The Bureau is not designed to replace diocesan initiative and activity nor to launch specific types of family movements, but it serves rather as a clearinghouse of information and an assisting agency for all family-life activities whether organized on a diocesan or a national basis.

Although it is difficult to classify the various family-life organizations operating throughout the country, we can clarify the over-all picture somewhat by indicating the principal types of activity that they are established to promote. These activities fall into two broad categories: the promotion of special sessions devoted to instruction and retreat, and the formation of groups or cells each composed of a limited number of couples who meet periodically for study, discussion, and apostolic action. Let us look at a few examples in each category.

The Cana Conference would fall primarily into the first classification. Its chief means of helping married couples is the conference. This is an all-day or half-day session held annually or semiannually to inspire, motivate, and instruct couples in Christian family living. During the conferences, instructions are given concerning family ideals, the sacramental nature of marriage, the rights and duties of husband and wife, the various aspects of marriage and family relationships, and other related subjects. Opportunity is offered for questions and discussion, and the conference usually closes with renewal of the marriage vows before or during Benediction of the Blessed Sacrament.[1]

The Pre-Cana Conference, on the other hand, is designed to help engaged couples prepare for a truly Christian marriage. Although the program differs in various dioceses, it typically consists of three or four conferences given on separate evenings by skilled directors from pertinent backgrounds such as a priest, a doctor or a nurse, and an experienced married couple. Some dioceses also sponsor lectures on dating and courtship for those who are not yet engaged. Along the same line some dioceses sponsor a series of mailed lessons or instructions for engaged couples. These substitute for the conferences and perhaps require somewhat less organization and manpower.[2]

Included in this first category also are the various organizations promoting retreats for married couples. An example is the enthusiastic Holy Family Retreat Association operating in Arizona, California, and Nevada. This is a lay-sponsored, ecclesiastically approved movement organized to promote married couples' retreats. Chapters of the Association are formed in various cities and serve to foster the movement in their area. A typical retreat begins Friday evening at 8:00 P.M. and ends with the renewal of marriage vows and informal assembly around 4:00 P.M. Sunday.[3] Spiritual directors in the Church

[1] For an example of Cana organization and thinking in one archdiocese, see *The New Cana Manual,* ed. by the Rev. Walter Imbiorski (Delaney Publications, 206 South Grove St., Oak Park, Ill., 1957).

[2] See *The Marriage Preparation Course* published by the Family Life Bureau of the National Catholic Welfare Conference.

[3] Information on this movement may be obtained from Holy Family Retreat Association, Arizona Chapter, 24 Marshall St., Phoenix, Ariz.

are unanimous in their belief that retreats offer a superior means of obtaining the knowledge and grace necessary to fulfill the obligations of one's state in life. The eager response that married couples' retreats have received wherever they have been offered strongly corroborates this belief. Obviously it will be some time before any considerable number of married couples will find it possible to make such retreats, but the need is there, and propitious beginnings have been made.

Examples of family organizations focusing primarily on activities that we have included in the second category, namely, the formation of functioning groups or cells, are the Christian Family Movement (CFM), the Association of Holy Family Guilds, and various diocesan-centered organizations such as the Family Federation of the Archdiocese of St. Paul. CFM is the largest of the modern family-life movements. It aims to restore Christian ideals in family life by working on the environment in which families live. The basic unit is composed of from four to eight couples who meet biweekly and use the familiar "inquiry" method of observing, judging, and acting to achieve their objective. The national Coordinating Committee of the movement, acting on the suggestions submitted from the various section committees throughout the country, prepares an annual "inquiry booklet" which furnishes material for the biweekly meetings to be held during the year. Major emphasis is placed on a different subject each year, for example, social responsibility, education, race relations, community, parish, and so forth.[4]

The Association of Holy Family Guilds originated in San Antonio and operates primarily in the state of Texas. A Guild is composed of from five to twelve couples and a priest who acts as spiritual moderator. Meetings are held twice each month, with one meeting devoted to brief business matters and to discussion bearing on some phase of Christian marriage or family life, and the other to strictly social activities. Hence the movement's program includes discussions—to increase personal knowledge of the Church and its teachings; projects—to ac-

[4] The national office of CFM is Room 2010, 100 West Monroe St., Chicago 3, Ill.

tually work on or with Catholic Action projects for the improvement of the community; and socials—to bring Catholic families together on a basis of friendship and hospitality.[5]

Since the basic unit of the Church's activity in family life is the diocese, many bishops have, according to felt need and available manpower, appointed diocesan family-life directors who have both the authority and responsibility to initiate activity within the diocese. Many of these have displayed admirable energy and ingenuity in devising programs to meet modern needs. In general they promote a wide variety of activities ranging through instruction in the schools, marriage preparation courses, Cana, parental guidance, marriage counseling, and so forth.

As one example of diocesan activity falling under the second category we have defined, we may consider the Family Federation of the Archdiocese of St. Paul. The Federation is composed of small groups or cells (five or six couples) who meet weekly in the home of each of the cell members on a rotational basis. Each of these couples has a group of other couples interested in the goals of Catholic Action to whom they transmit the results of each meeting. The Federation has a threefold goal: to renew the spiritual lives of husbands and wives—a work begun through special one-day retreats (Cana Days); to restore to families the basic values of our Christian heritage—here the "inquiry method" is employed; and to build a better world through the medium of better families.[6]

This spirited development of family programs and organizations—we have mentioned only a few—clearly responds to a series of needs recognized by both religious leaders and laity alike. What are these needs? Catholic couples want what may

[5] See *Association of Holy Family Guilds Manual*, P.O. Box 5181, Beacon Hill Station, San Antonio, Tex.

[6] See *Catholic Family Action*, a Handbook of Technique and Procedure, ed. by Chester and Mary Rank under the direction of the Rev. Richard T. Doherty (The Liturgical Press, St. John's Abbey, Collegeville, Minn., 1956).

be called a postgraduate course in marriage and family living. The formal religious training of many Catholics stops while they are relatively immature. Even those who receive college training in Catholic schools soon discover that their understanding and appreciation of Christian family values can be adequately developed only in the school of everyday experience. Formal religion classes at best can only provide the foundations upon which they must constantly build. Postgraduate training calls for the constant reappraisal of the meaning of the marriage vocation. Because Catholic couples are subjected to a variety of confusing and contradictory influences which tend to dull their keen perception of spiritual values, they recognize the need to rethink constantly the meaning of married life in terms of traditional Catholic principles *and* contemporary living conditions.

Catholic couples also feel the need to retain or regain their sense of unity with the Church. Humanly speaking, religious solidarity must be experienced through some concrete forms of interaction with other members of the group if it is to support and strengthen the individual's adherence to group standards. As Catholics become increasingly mobile, moving away from the traditional centers of solidarity associated with the communities of their youth, many find it difficult to identify with fellow Catholics in their new situations. Since their participation in the liturgy has been reduced to a more or less passive, perfunctory role, they experience little sense of unity in their weekly half-hour attendance at Mass.

Under these circumstances the constant, daily impact of secular attitudes and practices strikes many couples with peculiar force. They feel out of step with their neighbors, yet they experience little sense of unity with their fellow Catholics. After a time many discover that more or less unconsciously they are acquiring the secular outlooks and conduct of those around them. Hence, if they still cherish high Christian ideals they are eager to associate with other like-minded couples. The various family movements that are geared primarily to action serve as excellent social vehicles for promoting the desired solidarity, inasmuch as experience shows that people become aware of their unity chiefly by doing things together.

There is a further reason why couples feel the need for unity and solidarity. Catholic families are encountering many new situations calling for new solutions. These must be worked out within the Catholic framework of values. Individual couples find this difficult to manage alone and frequently are not sure whether they have the right solutions. Furthermore, if approved Catholic solutions call for considerable sacrifice because they differ markedly from those accepted in the secular culture, couples feel the need for the support and encouragement that come from associating with others who face the same problems.

We have indicated rather briefly the general character of the family-life activity initiated to meet modern needs. What remains to be done? Obviously in a complex, rapidly changing society new family needs will constantly arise, so that all family programs must retain flexibility, initiative, and ingenuity if they are to accomplish their long-range purposes. This means that the leaders of these movements must continuously and courageously deepen their understanding of pertinent principles, revaluate their methods, and re-examine the problems they should be meeting. Likewise, they must attract new members and make adequate provisions for their training and formation. Failure to absorb new members may cause the movement to be dominated by "vested interests" or a type of "mutual admiration" society. Failure to train and form new members adequately may result in rapid growth but loss, and even perversion, of the essential purposes of the movement.

These are typical problems which plague every organization. We have mentioned them only in passing, for our present purpose is to indicate some of the "unfinished business" that must be tackled next. Our selection does not aim to be exhaustive; rather, we have chosen to comment on a few problems that appear particularly pressing at the moment. Nor can our treatment be exhaustive. All that space allows is the mere delineation of the dimensions of the problem.

Throughout this work we have tended to focus attention on the special problems which Catholic families face because of their religious minority position, but we did not wish to imply that other factors producing marital instability leave Catholic couples unaffected. Pastors, doctors, lawyers, social workers, and marriage counselors testify that Catholics apparently have their fair share of marital problems. The few available studies on the cases handled by civil divorce courts and chancery offices point in the same direction. Although there is little agreement on the ultimate causal factors involved in the breakdown of marriage, our research indicates that the routine problems of drink, infidelity, desertion and non-support, irresponsibility, incompatibility, and so on, plague Catholic couples and threaten the stability of their marriages pretty much as they do all others. This means that a considerable number of families encounter problems that require competent outside assistance if marital failure is to be avoided.

Where can Catholic couples take their marital troubles? Studies show that in the past they turned to friends and relatives, their pastors or clerical friends, doctors, nurses, lawyers, teachers, social workers, and, more recently, professional marriage counselors. Clearly there are plenty of people willing to offer advice. Are they competent? With the possible exception of the clergy, social workers, and professional counselors, their competency can be questioned. Even among these latter groups Catholic couples may find far from adequate help. Professional marriage counselors are not always available and, furthermore, they may be of little assistance if they fail to understand and appreciate the Catholic viewpoint. Until recently the training of the majority of social workers has not been focused on marriage counseling, for their primary professional interests lay in other areas. In like manner the formal training of the clergy has tended to ignore this important aspect of pastoral care.

It follows that there is a real need to train competent marriage counselors. A start has been made at the Catholic University of America, which now offers special training in this area. Schools of social work would do well to reconsider present curriculum content in terms of the growing demand for social workers to engage in marriage counseling. Finally, efforts must be increased to prepare the clergy for more adequate skill in fulfilling this pastoral function. In the established structure of the Church it is the pastor and his assistants who should first handle cases of marital trouble in their parish. The helping professions—that is, social workers and trained marriage counselors—should be available for cases presenting special difficulties, but even these professionals can function adequately only if they work in close co-operation with the local pastor.

Another area calling for attention is the relationship between parents and the schools. In every stable society the family plays the essential role in the character formation of the coming generation. Modern parents are coming in for a good deal of criticism on this score. The increase of juvenile delinquency is arousing major national concern, and the apparent lack of parental control is frequently singled out as a basic cause. This accusation leaves parents somewhat perplexed. Only a short time ago child psychologists were warning them to be "permissive." Parental authority became a nasty word. At the same time educators were demanding that parents leave the training of youth to them. They grew quite impatient with parental "interference" in the educational process. Today it seems that parents are being blamed for taking the "experts" at their word. They have been permissive and they have trustingly confided their children to the schools.

Now, according to Catholic doctrine the primary, natural, and ordinarily irreplaceable school of religion and the moral virtues is the home. The principal—and natural—teachers of religion and morals are the parents. The school and the religious teacher can at best serve only as aids, not as substitutes, for the home and the parents in the adequate religious formation of the child. The practical implications of this doctrine have been overlooked by some parents and teachers alike. Many Catholic parents feel that they are fulfilling their obligations if they support the school and send their children to it. Many pastors and religious teachers conduct the schools as if parents had no other function than to supply the children and render financial support.

Hence, there is serious need for closer understanding and cooperation between parents, teachers, and religious directors of the schools. Briefly, this requires two things. In the first place, there must be a change of attitudes. All the parties involved must recognize that moral and religious training is a cooperative process in which parents hold the primary obligation, and teachers serve as delegated assistants. This means that parents, teachers, and religious leaders must work together in solving mutual problems and formulating practical programs.

At the same time, co-operation cannot be left to chance. Some type of formal organization must be established by means of which all the parties involved can come together to discuss their problems and be assured of adequate representation. This may imply the redefinition of some assumed pastoral and teacher prerogatives, as well as increased insistence on parental responsibility, but the present situation must be modified if the schools are to fulfill their function adequately under modern conditions.

In line with the problem above is the need for greater participation in community affairs. Catholic families, like all other families, must work out their way of life in a rapidly changing, pluralistic, industrialized urban environment. They consequently face not only the same family difficulties as others, but many problems related to juvenile delinquency, housing, slum clearance, public health, race relations, public morals, and so forth can be solved only through united community action. It follows that Catholics must co-operate with all other citizens of good will in attempting to meet their common needs. This obligation is clear, and in theory it should be relatively easy for Catholics to work out co-operation with others since the Catholic viewpoint is based on the order of reason, which can be recognized by all men of good will. This is to say that although Catholics maintain that the supernatural completely transcends the natural order it does not destroy it. The right use of creatures is discovered by studying the nature of things in their normal operations, so that even those who do not accept the Catholic view of the supernatural can accept the Catholic view of the natural.

However, there are numerous obstacles to co-operation in practice. Adequate means of discussion and communication between Catholics and others do not always exist, with the result that programs that should have common support are neglected because they are labeled Catholic or non-Catholic in origin. Co-operation sometimes fails because representatives of one or all of the groups involved do not clearly understand the implications of their own beliefs and consequently reject what they should logically support. Furthermore, co-operation in a pluralistic society sometimes requires compromise in working out practical programs of action, on the principle that half a loaf is better than none. Such situations demand understanding and tact but present no insurmountable obstacles provided all parties sincerely seek the best interests of the community. It follows that co-operation requires people trained in human relations and leadership. Among Catholics perhaps one of the most fruitful results of Catholic Action and the various family movements will be the formation of such competent persons.

A final area calling for greater concern in the future is public policy and the family. If the maintenance of healthy family life is as important for society as we all assume, then conditions which hinder the family from functioning successfully must be matters of public concern. Following a century of almost total neglect the past few decades have witnessed a growing awareness of basic family needs. Various types of direct and indirect assistance to dependent children and needy families have been introduced, some attempts at slum clearance and the provision of adequate housing have been initiated, and there are hopeful though limited indications that the exploitation of racial minorities will be moderated. On the other hand, the income status of the nation's child-rearing families is far from satisfactory. A report prepared by the Children's Bureau, Social Security Administration, Department of Health, Education, and Welfare, for the Joint Committee on the Economic Report offers some pertinent information concerning children and low-income families.

For example, in 1954 children under twenty-one years numbered 59,300,000. Low-income families carried a disproportionate share of the responsibility for rearing these children. As of 1954, families with three or more children under eighteen years of age constituted only 18 per cent of all families, but they were rearing 54 per cent of the country's children. Likewise, families with four or more children constituted only 8 per cent of all families, but they had 30 per cent of the nation's children. In general, families with large numbers of children received lower than average incomes although they faced greater demands in terms of child support. For example, as compared with a national average family income of $4,173, families supporting four children received an average income of only $3,949; families with five children $3,155; and families with six children or more, $3,252.

In the light of these figures Americans might well consider whether some type of family allowance should not be granted to parents who bear the burden of raising the nation's children. As used here the term *family allowance* represents a cash payment to the family, the amount based upon the number and age of the children. Practically all the countries on the continent of Europe, together with the United Kingdom, Ireland, Australia, New Zealand, Canada, Chile, Uruguay, and Lebanon, have maintained a system of family allowances for some time. Their programs are not based solely on the financial inadequacy of some families to provide for their children; rather, they represent attempts to widen the basis of child support, to distribute more equitably the costs of maintaining the nation's children, to equalize the opportunities between children with respect to their start in life, and to increase the children's share of the total national income.

These programs merit more serious study and consideration than they have received in the past. Some have attempted to dismiss them on the grounds that they were little more than programs to raise the birth rate. Considering the variety of factors that influence this rate, no serious student of the problem would attempt to sustain this contention. Likewise, some labor leaders have been cool to such programs because they fear it will have adverse effects upon wages. The experience of nations operating such programs should allay this fear. Some leaders feel that there are other, better ways of achieving the same objectives. This is a legitimate position, but they must prove their sincerity by offering better ways to meet the problem. All too often in the past, opposition to social reforms on the basis that there were better ways of handling the situation were merely smoke screens thrown up to avoid facing the issue.

To conclude, the rapid growth and extension of a wide variety of family movements and activities show that Catholic couples are meeting the challenge of modern society with energy and acumen. Cana conferences and family retreats serve to deepen their understanding and appreciation of the sacramental bond, while co-operation in family movements strengthens their feeling of solidarity and enables them to proceed as a group in tackling common problems. Some unfinished business remains, but as insights are deepened and leaders are formed we have every reason to expect that adequate programs will be developed in all areas.

There have been and will continue to be serious losses under the steady impact of secularism. The fulfillment of the Catholic ideal of marriage involves the acceptance of a total philosophy of life based on the faithful imitation and following of Christ. Apparently some are unable to accept it, while others grow confused and fail to grasp its implications in their conduct. Catholics who would maintain their family ideals intact must possess adequate knowledge, motivation, and unity, for the steady pressure to conform to the dominant culture can be withstood only by those who fully understand and appreciate their unique privilege of membership in the Mystical Body of Christ.